CAMBRIDGE SOCIAL BIOLOGY TOPICS

Series editors
S. Tyrell Smith and Alan Cornwell

HUMAN PHYSICAL HEALTH

Dennis Taylor

Head of Biology
Strode's Sixth Form College
Egham

CAMBRIDGE
UNIVERSITY PRESS

SEC

Published by the Press Syndicate of the University of Cambridge
The Pitt Building, Trumpington Street, Cambridge CB2 1RP
40 West 20th Street, New York, NY 10011–4211, USA
10 Stamford Road, Oakleigh, Melbourne 3166, Australia

© Cambridge University Press 1989

First published 1989
Sixth printing 1996

Printed in Great Britain at the University Press, Cambridge

British Library cataloguing in publication data

Taylor, Dennis
  Human physical health.
  1. Man. Diseases – For schools.
  I. Title
  616

ISBN 0 521 31306 6

Cover photo by Jeremy Hartley/OXFAM

SE

Contents

Preface

The control of disease and the active encouragement of good health is a major priority of nations worldwide, recognised by the setting up of the World Health Organisation in 1948. In Britain, for example, about 6% of our Gross National Product (the nation's wealth) is spent on the National Health Service. In this book a number of diseases and health problems are selected for detailed study. They are chosen for their importance, for the perspective they give on the problems of people in both developed and developing countries, and to represent the different causes of disease and health problems.

Despite the variety of problems, and hence the variety of strategies for tackling these problems, certain common themes and underlying principles emerge. For example, there is always the balance between social change and medical intervention to consider in alleviating disease; methods of transmission are limited and similar methods require similar strategies for control (compare, for example, cholera and *Salmonella*); some diseases are infectious and others are not; prevention is better than cure. It is these principles, requiring an understanding of both social and biological factors, which it is hoped will emerge in this book.

1 Health and disease – some basic principles

1.1 The concepts of health and disease

The World Health Organisation has defined **health** as 'a state of complete physical, mental and social well-being and not merely the absence of disease or infirmity'. In other words, for a person to be healthy, all parts of the body should be functioning efficiently, and the person should also **feel** well in body and mind. The term **disease** is less easy to define. In its broadest sense it could be taken to describe any disorder of normal bodily function and, like health, it has physical, mental and social dimensions. We can recognise these dimensions in the following examples:

physical disease	e.g. arteriosclerosis, dental caries (tooth decay)
mental illness/disease	e.g. depression, schizophrenia
social disease	e.g. alcoholism and other drug addiction, cardiovascular disease, malnutrition

In attempting to classify diseases further, the following categories are commonly used:

1 Diseases caused by other living organisms. Among these are the infectious or communicable diseases which are caused by micro-organisms, e.g. influenza, cholera.
2 'Human-induced' diseases, e.g. lung cancer, asbestosis, lead poisoning.
3 Degenerative diseases, e.g. ageing, arthritis, arteriosclerosis.
4 Inherited diseases, e.g. phenylketonuria, haemophilia, Down's syndrome.
5 Deficiency diseases, e.g. scurvy, kwashiorkor, rickets.
6 Mental illness.

The point that emerges is that it is almost impossible to define disease precisely, and that there are no rigid boundaries between the disease categories we conventionally recognise. For example, a genetic predisposition to a certain disease, such as stomach ulcers or cancer, may combine with occupational or dietary factors to trigger the appearance of the disease. Another factor of importance, which is as yet only beginning to be explored, is the relationship between the mind and the body in disease.

1.2 Worldwide distribution of disease

When the distribution of disease worldwide is considered, it is clear that a gulf exists between 'developed' and 'developing' countries. The developed countries are located mainly in the northern hemisphere (the 'North') and include the industrialised nations of Europe, N. America, the U.S.S.R., Japan, Australia and New Zealand. The developing countries (the 'South') are often referred to as 'Third World' countries and include the countries of Africa, Central and S. America, and Asia, excluding the U.S.S.R. and Japan. About 75% of the world's population is located in the developing countries. The different distribution of disease between developed and developing countries is obvious when the data in tables 1.1 and 1.2 and fig. 1.1 are compared. Reliable data are often unavailable from developing countries, but rough estimates can be made.

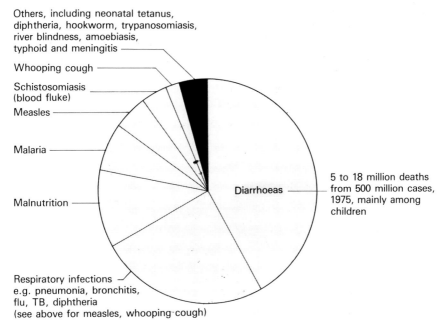

Figure 1.1 Estimates of mortality due to the major infectious diseases and malnutrition in Africa, Asia and Latin America 1977–78, from *The Health of Nations* Open University (1985) based on J. Walsh and K. Warren, selective primary health care in *New England Journal of Medicine* vol. 301, 1979; AIDS now ranks about tenth in Africa. Note: data on non-infectious diseases often not available

Note that fig. 1.1 merely shows the relative importance of different **infectious** diseases and malnutrition. Table 1.3 shows the reduction in **mortality** from some notifiable infectious diseases in England and Wales over the 50 year period 1930 to 1980. Note that the *incidence* of these diseases has not necessarily been reduced in exactly the same manner because in most cases, as with typhoid, modern treatment is much more effective, so more people recover.

Table 1.1 The five major causes of death in the UK, 1982. (OPCS, 1984, Table 3).

Cause of death	% of all deaths
coronary heart disease	32
cancers	23
respiratory disease	15
strokes	12
accidents	3
other causes	15

Table 1.2 Years of healthy life lost* in Ghana due to different diseases (excluding prematurity, birth injury and tetanus of the newborn, neonatal respiratory disease, pregnancy complications, congenital malformation).

Rank order	Disease	% of total healthy life lost
1	malaria	15.4
2	sickle-cell disease	6.2
3	measles	6.2
4	pneumonia (child)	5.5
5	malnutrition	5.1
6	gastroenteritis (diarrhoea)	4.5
7	accidents (all kinds)	2.9
8	tuberculosis	2.7
9	stroke**	2.4
10	pneumonia (adult)	2.3
11	psychiatric disorders	2.2
12	cirrhosis	1.3
13	cancer	1.2
14	hypertension (high blood pressure**)	1.2

*   Years of healthy life lost, NOT % of all deaths as in **Table 1.1**. If an accident killed someone at age 20 in a country where life expectancy is 70 years, 50 years of healthy life are lost. Accidents are more common in the young and hence accidents are given greater weight than cancer, which tends to kill later in life, compared with **Table 1.1**. The 3 highest contributors to years of healthy life lost in Canada (a developed country) are: accidents 38.9%, circulatory diseases 24.3% and cancer 15.7%.
**   Circulatory diseases.

Table 1.3 Changes in numbers of deaths from certain infections in England and Wales between 1930 and 1980. Based on data from *Lecture Notes on the Infectious Diseases*, 4th ed., Mandal, B.K. & Mayon-White, R.T., Blackwell Scientific Publications Ltd (1984).

Disease	Deaths in 1930	Deaths in 1980
measles	4188	26
diphtheria	3497	0
whooping cough	2037	6
scarlet fever	740	0
meningococcal infection (bacterial meningitis)	632	71
typhoid and paratyphoid	313	1
polio	164	0
dysentery	97	5
smallpox	28	0

In developed countries, communicable (infectious) diseases have, relatively recently, largely been brought under control due to improvements in nutrition, hygiene, housing, preventive medicine and treatment. As a result the average life expectancy has been increased and diseases associated with the degenerative changes of ageing have begun to assume more importance in the statistics. These *non*-infectious diseases are influenced by other factors, often self-inflicted, such as diet, life style, genetic predisposition and exposure to harmful conditions, and the methods of control differ accordingly as will become clear in later chapters.

Dr Halfdan Mahler, former Director General of the World Health Organisation (WHO), said in a speech marking the fortieth anniversary of WHO in 1988, that 'the tragedy of the health situation in the industrialised countries is the knowledge that so much of the disease, the disability, the suffering, the mental despair, the premature deaths, **all** of it is actually preventable.' The WHO is currently trying to promote a new health culture in industrialised countries which gets away from the old preaching style of telling people what to do and what not to do, and blaming them for indulging in health-damaging activities such as smoking, and moves towards a positive approach to health. This 'health promotion' is meant to be a grass-roots movement based firmly in the community with emphasis on people helping themselves. Environmental improvements will hopefully go hand in hand with health promotion. Many issues are politically sensitive (e.g. tobacco, food and drink industries, marketing of some drugs such as tranquilisers, lead in petrol) and it may be that politically sensitive changes will have to be brought about in response to community pressure, i.e. from the bottom up. 'Heartbeat Wales' and the 'Healthy Cities' project, which involves a number of European cities including Liverpool, are examples of health promotion in action.

Developing countries are faced with problems that have only recently been largely overcome by the developed countries. It is salutary to remember, for example, that typhoid and cholera were still widespread in Britain until the improvement in sanitation and water supplies that came with the Public Health Act of 1875. Clean, freshly available water and improved nutrition are probably the two most important factors which could reduce the incidence of infectious disease in developing countries, and these are accordingly top priorities for the World Health Organisation.

As fig. 1.1 shows, one of the world's worst killer diseases is malaria (see Chapter 4). Diseases resulting in diarrhoea are also important (see fig. 1.1). Undernourished children are far more at risk than well fed children and this is true of other diseases. Measles, for example, is a major killer if resistance to disease is low. Infections with other organisms such as parasitic worms or flukes, or secondary infections also reduce resistance. Diseases causing diarrhoea are commonly due to poor public hygiene and stem from contaminated water or food.

Respiratory infections are also major killers world-wide (see fig. 1.1). Until recently smallpox was another major killer, but this was eradicated in 1977 (see section 5.8). AIDS is likely to become a major killer disease in the near future.

1.3   Epidemiology and vital statistics

Epidemiology can be defined as the study of all factors which affect disease. It involves identifying the cause of the disease and all the factors which contribute to its appearance in a given population, e.g. age, sex, occupation, environment, living conditions, etc.

The data obtained are used to try to prevent the disease and to control its spread. To this end, the more serious infectious diseases are compulsorily **notifiable**, so that central records can be kept of outbreaks. In addition, all countries are encouraged by the World Health Organisation to keep a record of certain **vital statistics** on population, including **mortality** (deaths and causes of death) and **morbidity** (illness, including disease, injuries and disabilities). Note that mortality is concerned with the proportion of people dying from a given disease and that morbidity is concerned with the incidence of disease, whether it is fatal or not. Complete records of morbidity (incidence) are harder to obtain since not all cases are likely to be reported, even if notifiable diseases. In Britain, a Census is carried out every 10 years. The next is due in 1991.

Some of the statistical measures used, together with their advantages and limitations, are considered briefly below.

Crude death rate and crude birth rate

Crude death rate is the total number of deaths per year per thousand people in a population. The total population is taken as the mid-year figure. The highest rates occur in developing countries. In 1980, for example, the crude death rate was 16 for Africa compared with 8 for N. America. However, it was also 8 for Latin America, which may seem surprising because the latter contains many poor, developing countries. This highlights one of the dangers of using crude death rates alone, a problem discussed further below.

Crude birth rate is the total number of births per year per thousand people in a population. The crude birth rate for Latin America was roughly double that of N. America in 1980 (31 compared with 16). Hence there is a much higher proportion of young people in Latin America, with a consequent reduction in the *proportion* of people dying from old age and degenerative diseases. The large number of people being born each year tends to mask the number dying each year when crude death rates are being calculated, since the total population for a year includes all the live births of that year. The overall effect is that North and Latin America share similar crude death rates, but with very different socioeconomic and medical explanations. It is important therefore to consider the age distributions of populations, which is conventionally done by means of **population pyramids**, (see, for example, *Individuals and Populations*, P. Gadd, another book in this series). Crude birth rate minus crude death rate gives **rate of population growth**.

Infant mortality rate

Infant mortality rate is the number of deaths of infants under the age of one year per thousand live births. It is a sensitive and useful guide to living conditions, the level of socioeconomic development and public hygiene.

In 1982, infant mortality rate was 11 for England and Wales and 7 for Sweden and Japan. In the poorest countries it often exceeds 100, for example 215 in Sierra Leone (1981), 130 in Malawi (1981). It is easier to collect reliable information for infant mortality rate than for crude death rate and it can serve as a useful indicator of the state of public health in general. Infant mortality also generally correlates well with adult mortality.

Age-specific and sex-specific death rates

Two other useful mortality rates are the **age-specific death rate** and the **sex-specific death rate**. The age-specific death rate is the number of people of a given age group who die per year per thousand *of that age group*, e.g.

$$\frac{\text{no. of people aged 60 to 64}}{\text{total no. of people aged 60 to 64}} \times 1000$$

Since sex also affects the chances of dying, such figures are even more useful if calculated separately for the two sexes, e.g.

$$\frac{\text{no. of women aged 60 to 64}}{\text{total no. of women aged 60 to 64}} \times 1000$$

These figures are likely to give more reliable comparisons than overall crude death rates because they take into account the important differences that occur with age or sex. For example, the crude death rate from cancer in England and Wales is much higher now than 100 years ago but the age-specific rates for all cancers combined (excluding lung cancer) are similar. The change in crude death rate is due mainly to a higher proportion of old people in the population. It was noted above that North America and Latin America have similar crude death rates. However, the age-specific death rates are higher for Latin America.

Standardised mortality ratio (SMR)

The standardised mortality ratio (SMR) is a means of comparing a particular section of the population with a standardised mortality rate. Thus, if the overall death rate for England in 1968 is set at 100, SMR for England in 1980 was 87, indicating that the death rate in 1980 was 87% of that in 1968. Normally, for any given period, SMR for a whole country or population is, by definition, 100.

$$\text{SMR} = \frac{\text{observed deaths}}{\text{deaths in standard population}} \times 100$$

A ratio is thus obtained between observed deaths and the standard chosen. This is converted to a percentage. SMR is usually calculated on an age-specific basis, using age-specific death rates for the standard population, (the standard being the total population of the country).

Thus it would be possible to record the number of deaths from coronary heart disease nationwide for each age group and obtain a total figure. Londoners could then be compared by taking into account the age structure of the London population and calculating the *expected* number of deaths for each group based on the standard (national) figures. *Actual* London deaths would then be expressed as a percentage of this. For lung cancer in females, SMR was 159 in England in 1980 compared with 100 in 1968, a significant increase in the relative importance of lung cancer as a cause of death in females.

1.4 Socioeconomic factors in disease

In recent years, the common view that the dramatic decline in infectious diseases in developing countries over the last 150 years has been due to medical intervention has been challenged, and a more balanced picture, which includes the importance of social and economic factors, has emerged. In this context, the information given in fig. 1.2 is interesting. Although medical intervention appears to have had a decisive effect in virtually eliminating diphtheria and smallpox (as it has for polio), significant declines in tuberculosis, whooping cough and measles were underway long before medical intervention in the form of vaccination or chemotherapy (drug/antibiotic treatment). This has been highlighted by Professor McKeown, formerly Professor of Social Medicine at Birmingham University. It shows that we must do more than look to medical intervention if patterns of disease are to be changed. The improvements in hygiene of water and sanitation that accompanied the introduction of the **Public Health Act 1875** were vital, but Professor McKeown argues that improved living standards, particularly better nutrition, have been even more important because they resulted in increased *resistance* to disease. Other factors identified as important are less overcrowding, which reduces the opportunity for infectious diseases to spread as rapidly, and better personal hygiene. Education is an important contributor to the latter.

The biosocial implications of this viewpoint are important because it suggests that social, economic and behavioural factors are sometimes more important than medical factors in controlling disease. Since prevention of disease rather than cure is preferred, we must consider very carefully how to allocate resources in the future.

One line of inquiry which highlights the importance of socioeconomic factors is a study of health differences between the social classes. In 1977, the Secretary of State for Social Services set up such an inquiry under the chairmanship of Sir Douglas Black, the former president of the Royal College of Physicians. **The Black Report** was published in 1980 and has been a source of much controversy ever since. The Report showed the inequalities that existed between the social classes, that these inequalities had persisted ever since the introduction of the NHS and were, in some cases, getting greater.

The Registrar General divides the population of England and Wales into six social classes based on the occupation of the chief wage earner of the family (see table 1.4) and on every death certificate occupation is recorded.

Some of the findings of the Black Report were:

1 People from class V (unskilled manual) had a 2.5 times greater chance of dying before retirement age than those from class I (professional/managerial).

2 During the first month of life a baby from class V is twice as likely to die as one from class I, representing excess deaths of about 3000–4000 babies per year.

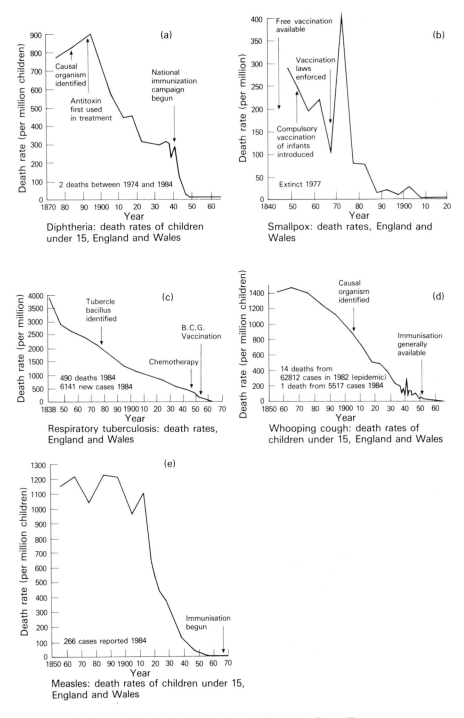

Figure 1.2 Death rates in England and Wales from (a) diphtheria, (b) smallpox, (c) tuberculosis, (d) whooping cough and (e) measles, from T. McKeown *The Modern Rise of Population* Edward Arnold (1976)

13

3 Manual workers suffer a higher incidence of the major diseases such as cancer and heart disease.
4 Morbidity rates are far higher in classes IV and V than in class I.
5 Mortality rates for men aged 35−54 have increased in classes IV and V over the last 30 years.

Table 1.4 Social classes of England and Wales (Registrar General's classification).

Non-Manual	
Class I	professional occupations (lawyers, doctors etc.).
Class II	managerial and lower professional occupations (e.g. teachers, nurses, sales managers).
Class III N	non-manual skilled occupations (clerks, shop assistants).
Manual	
Class III M	skilled manual occupations (bricklayers, underground coal miners etc.
Class IV	partly skilled occupations (bus conductors, postmen etc.).
Class V	unskilled occupations (porters, labourers etc.).

Table 1.5 illustrates variations in mortality with social class for certain common causes of death. The figures on Occupational Mortality published in July 1986 showed that although, overall, health was improving for everyone, that of manual workers was improving less rapidly than that of non-manual workers. This is shown by the SMR which emphasises the **relative** health of the two groups. The SMR for unskilled men in social class V rose from 137 to 165 during the 1970s and early 1980s but had dropped for men in social class I from 77 to 66. It can also be argued from the figures (see *New Scientist*, 6 Nov 1986, 65) that the unemployed have a relatively high SMR.

Figures based on Occupational Mortality have been criticised for the following reasons:
  (i) they exclude anyone under the age of 15
 (ii) they exclude retired people
(iii) they exclude all women
(iv) class V has shrunk in size
 (v) people often change class and it is the healthy who tend to move up and unhealthy who tend to move down.

Nevertheless the figures are worth studying. Another interesting source of information is a 'longitudinal study', started with the Census of 1971, in which details of everyone born on four particular days of that year (the dates are secret) will be followed throughout their lives. This will be done by studying birth certificates, death certificates and Census returns.

It is difficult to identify all the reasons for the differences in mortality between different social classes. Poverty, bad housing, poor working and living conditions, poor education all seem to contribute to poor health. It has been shown that material deprivation and poor environment are even more closely correlated with poor health than occupational class. Also, the middle and upper

Table 1.5 Standardised mortality ratio by cause and social class, England and Wales, 1970–72. SMR of 100 is average. (From Occupational Mortality England and Wales 1970–72, OPCS.)

Cause	Social Class					
	I	II	III N	III M	IV	V
all causes (men)	77	81	99	106	114	137
all causes (women)	82	87	92	115	119	135
ischaemic heart disease (men)	88	91	114	107	108	111
cancer of lung (men)	53	68	84	118	123	143
cancer of breast (women)	117	112	110	109	103	92
cancer of cervix uteri	44	66	69	120	140	161
suicide (women)	124	110	118	83	87	94

classes tend to be more aware of, and make better use of, available facilities. The main problem is not so much one of unequal treatment of disease, as unequal risks in the first place. Factors other than those mentioned are probably also operating. Why, for example, does class II have poorer health than class I?

A general consensus is emerging that more attention should be focused on poor living conditions, housing, poverty, education and occupational and environmental health hazards. Within the medical sphere, there ought perhaps to be less emphasis on curative medicine, which tends to be expensive high-technology, hospital-based medicine, and more emphasis on primary health care in the community (largely preventive medicine). This could require more health centres, health visitors and community nurses. The decisions that have to be taken are social, economic and political as well as medical. Effective screening programmes, for example, for cervical or breast cancer, although expensive to set up, may save money in the long term quite apart from the reduction in suffering and loss of life that result (see section 1.5 **Early Diagnosis**). Education of the public in basic health issues such as diet, how to cope with stress, the dangers of drugs such as alcohol and tobacco, the importance of exercise, the dangers of sexually transmitted disease, pre-natal care, immunisation, is another important area where preventive action is possible.

All these considerations apply to developing countries as well as developed countries, perhaps to an even greater degree. Primary health care workers work in the community and the service they provide is meant to be cheap to run and available to everybody. They deal with basic health care.

1.5   Principles of control: prevention and treatment

There are two aspects of control, namely **prevention** and **treatment**. The well-known saying 'Prevention is better than cure' is true not only on the basis of reducing suffering, but on economic grounds. However, prevention is not always possible, and the correct way to go about prevention is not always obvious, as became clear in section 1.4. In this book the distinction between treatment and prevention will be stressed, and treatment will be taken to mean the remedial process that is started once a person has contracted a disease.

Certain basic *medical* principles have emerged over the last century as to how to tackle disease. Some of these principles are stated below, and their application is illustrated by reference to particular diseases in chapters 2, 3, 4, 7 and 8.

Certain diseases illustrate certain principles particularly well. Typhoid and salmonella, for example, illustrate the importance of tracing carriers and contacts; malaria illustrates the importance of understanding the life cycle of the infective agent and of devising methods to interrupt the life cycle. Smallpox, polio and diphtheria illustrate the importance of immunisation. It is interesting to see how established principles are being applied to the relatively new disease AIDS, which is considered in chapter 3. In studying a particular disease, bear in mind not just the details of the disease but remember to think about which *general* principles of control are illustrated.

Causative agent

The causative agent of a disease is the organism that is the direct cause of the disease. The causative agent of malaria, for example, is a unicellular organism (a protozoan) called *Plasmodium*. It is transmitted by the mosquito but the latter is termed a **vector** and is not the causative agent. Identification of the causative agent is an important step in planning strategies of control. It allows certain predictions to be made about its behaviour, since this will differ markedly for viruses, bacteria, protozoans, fungi etc.

Method of transmission

Diseases which can spread from one person to another are generally called **communicable** or **infectious diseases**. Most infectious diseases are **airborne** (spread by droplet infection), **faecal borne** (spread by faecal contamination of water, food, utensils, etc) or spread by **direct contact** from animals (**vectors**) or humans. In the latter category, sexually transmitted diseases are the largest and most important group. Examples of all these modes of transmission will be given later. Once the method of transmission of a disease is known, appropriate, and in many cases standard, preventive measures can hopefully be applied, given the right socioeconomic and political conditions.

Signs and symptoms

An individual suffering from a particular disease will show certain characteristic signs and symptoms typical of that disease. **Signs** are characteristics that are detectable by another person, such as a doctor. They include such things as fever, rashes, diarrhoea, swollen glands, presence of a virus in blood samples. A **symptom** is an experience felt by the patient which has no physical expression, e.g. headache, pain, soreness of limbs, depression, fatigue, nausea. Signs and symptoms are sometimes jointly referred to as the **clinical features** of a disease. The term symptom is often used in a looser sense to include both signs and symptoms. However, in this book, the distinction between signs and symptoms is kept so that it can be left to the discretion of the reader whether or not to follow this policy.

Early diagnosis

Signs and symptoms are important in the early diagnosis of disease. The earlier a diagnosis is made, the more effective control measures are likely to be. Early diagnosis is therefore one of the main weapons we have against disease. It is particularly important with certain diseases, such as cervical and breast cancer, which can be cured much more reliably in their early stages (see below). Screening programmes for cancer operate on this principle. In the case of some inherited diseases, early diagnosis may allow a disease to be identified in a foetus, and the option of abortion to be considered (see below). Early diagnosis can be equally important with infectious diseases. For example, **onchoceriasis**, or 'river blindness', affects about 40 million people in tropical areas. It is caused by primitive worms known as **filarial worms** similar to the worms that cause elephantiasis. Recently it has become possible to detect filarial antigens in the body fluids of patients and early treatment with newly developed drugs may cure the condition before its effects become significant.

Monoclonal antibodies (see section 5.11) are the basis for an increasing number of diagnostic kits, as for Chaga's disease, a major tropical disease caused by a South American trypanosome (a protozoan).

Screening for cervical cancer and breast cancer

Within the U.K. there is currently much controversy over the application of techniques for early diagnosis. A classic example has been **cervical cancer**. Official statistics reveal an alarming increase in the number of deaths from the disease, with about 2000 deaths per year being recorded. If detected early by a cervical smear (a well-established screening technique in which a few cells scraped from the cervix are examined in a laboratory) a complete cure can usually be effected very rapidly. In Scandinavia, for example, the disease is now rare. A recently introduced method of treatment is the use of a laser beam to burn away very precisely the affected area of the cervix, causing minimal damage to surrounding tissues. This technique is quick, painless (it is done under local anaesthetic) and relatively easy to perform, and can even be done in the outpatients' department of a hospital. The cure rate is over 90%. Those parts of the country, such as the north east, where screening services have been poor have the highest death rates. Women over 35 years old and those of lower socioeconomic classes are most at risk. Despite government plans introduced in 1987 to improve the screening service, a lack of staff and facilities means that the service is still not as efficient as it could be.

Breast cancer is one of the most common types of cancer in women, occurring in about 1 in 20. If diagnosed early, prospects for cure are good. Untreated, the disease will prove fatal. Education of women to feel for unusual lumps in the breast, and X-ray screening (mammography) are techniques for early diagnosis.

Pre-natal diagnosis (early detection of foetal abnormality)

The birth of a severely handicapped baby is not only an emotional shock, but has long-term consequences for the family involved which may be economic as well as emotional and social. About 3% of babies born in the U.K. suffer some kind of abnormality. The majority of these abnormalities are treatable, but increasingly such conditions are becoming preventable. Early detection of foetal abnormality may allow a mother or couple to decide to opt for abortion, or it may lead in some cases to remedial action, thus minimising or preventing long-term damage. This is a rapidly growing area of medicine due to recent advances in obtaining samples of foetal material and in genetics and gene manipulation. Some of the current and possible future techniques are discussed below.

1 Amniocentesis

This is usually offered to older women (late 30s or 40 +) since they have a higher risk of having a baby with Down's syndrome, or those at risk from a particular genetic disease such as spina bifida. It is usually carried out in the 16th week of pregnancy (14th to 17th week possible) and involves removal of a small sample of amniotic fluid by insertion of a long, thin, hollow needle through the wall of the abdomen into the uterus. A local anaesthetic is applied and it is usually accompanied by an ultrasound scan (see below) to confirm the position of the foetus. There is a roughly 0.5 to 1% chance of miscarriage. The amniotic fluid contains cells which have been cast off from the amnion and the baby's skin, respiratory and digestive tracts. The cells are cultured (grown and multiplied) and eventually their chromosomes examined, the procedure taking 3 weeks. Major chromosomal abnormalities, such as Down's syndrome, in which the foetus shows 47 chromosomes instead of the normal 46, can be detected. The woman or couple can then be offered an abortion. The amniotic fluid is also tested chemically for alpha-fetoprotein (AFP). A higher than normal level of this liver protein would indicate spina bifida or other neural tube defects. The diagnosis can often be confirmed by ultrasound scanning (see below). The protein AFP is also detectable in the mother's blood from 18 weeks of pregnancy and a positive result can be confirmed by amniocentesis.

Certain genes are known to cause 'inborn errors of metabolism', such as phenylketonuria (PKU), usually associated with production of an abnormal enzyme or protein. The foetal cells can be tested for the products of some of these faulty genes and about 100 of the roughly 600 known diseases can now be identified at this stage.

2 Chorionic villus sampling (CVS) or chorionic biopsy

This technique was developed in China in 1975 and introduced into the U.K. in the early 1980s. It is an alternative to amniocentesis and has the advantage that it is done much earlier, typically at about 9 weeks into pregnancy (6 to 9 weeks possible). Results are known within a few days because the chorionic villi contain large numbers of dividing cells. A small sample of tissue is removed from the early placenta, a structure called the chorion which has many projections called villi. It is still a specialist technique and carries a higher risk of miscarriage than amniocentesis (about 4 to 5%), so is available at only a few hospitals. It cannot detect neural tube defects. A nationwide trial is currently going on in the U.K. comparing the short- and long-term risks with amniocentesis, and the technique should become more widely available in the future.

3 Ultrasound scans

In this technique a beam of inaudible sound waves of high frequency (20 to several thousand kHz) is aimed at the foetus and the echoes (reflections) are converted electronically to a picture on a monitor screen. The intensity of reflection (or absorption) depends on the density of the reflecting structure and interfaces between different tissues can therefore be visualised. In this way certain structures of the foetus can be measured and examined:

(i) maximum diameter of head
  – indicates stage of pregnancy and allows prediction of delivery date
  – detection of abnormality, e.g. hydrocephalus (excess fluid in the brain causing swelling)
(ii) physical defects e.g. spina bifida (see amniocentesis)
(iii) body size – check on normal body growth
(iv) bones and heart visible, including heart chamber
(v) position of placenta – important later in pregnancy e.g. if placenta lies across exit of uterus a Caesarean section may be needed at delivery
(vi) opaque placenta may indicate a 'Rhesus baby'
(vii) multiple pregnancies detected
(viii) ectopic pregnancy (growth of foetus outside uterus) detected
(ix) breech presentation detected

4 DNA analysis (analysis of restriction fragment length polymorphisms or RFLPs)

A technique which is likely to prove useful in the future is analysis of the DNA of foetal cells. In this way, single gene defects like those causing cystic fibrosis, Huntington's chorea and other genetic diseases will be detectable. The technique involves 'chopping up' a DNA sample with enzymes called **restriction enzymes** which act like scissors, and each of which chops the DNA only at locations which have specific base sequences. If the base sequence of a gene has been changed (a mutation), as with genetic diseases, the relevant piece of DNA will be chopped into pieces (**restriction fragments**) of different lengths in the normal and abnormal cells. The fragments are said to show polymorphism (variable form). The lengths for a particular disease will be characteristic of that disease.

5 Embryo biopsy

Pre-implantation diagnosis of disease should become possible in the near future if the techniques of *in vitro* fertilisation (IVF) are combined with embryo biopsy. With IVF, fertilisation takes place outside the woman's body in a dish in the laboratory and the resulting zygote is allowed to grow to the stage of a small embryo. Before the embryo is implanted in the woman it is anticipated that it will be possible to remove one cell from the small ball of cells without damaging the embryo and to use this cell for chromosomal and genetic analysis.

Other techniques for early diagnosis

A number of more familiar diagnostic tests are used routinely such as X-rays, blood tests and urine tests. Two newer techniques worthy of mention are fibre optic endoscopy and CAT scans.

Fibre optic endoscopy An endoscope is an instrument which allows a direct view of internal organs. A modified version of the instrument has allowed major advances in early diagnosis by allowing cavities of the body to be explored which could formerly be explored only by major surgery. The endoscope is combined with fibre optics by attaching a flexible lighted tube about 1 cm in diameter. The tube contains fibres which transmit light along the lengths even when bent and curved round corners. At the tip of the tube (inside the body) is an objective lens. At the other end (the viewing end outside the body) is an eyepiece lens with focus controls and a camera attachment. The tube is pushed into formerly inaccessible parts of the body such as lungs, intestines, heart, knee joints and the abdominal cavity, if necessary with local or general anaesthetic. Early diagnosis of some ulcers, cancers, blockages and so on is possible. The **laparoscope** is a type of endoscope used to examine the abdominal organs, including the female reproductive organs, for example when removing 'eggs' for IVF or for detecting blocked Fallopian tubes in infertility investigations.

CAT scans With computerised axial tomography (CAT) a 'dye' which is opaque to X-rays is injected into the blood and X-rays passed in all directions through the part of the body being examined. This allows visualisation of soft tissues. The X-rays are recorded, processed by a computer and a picture produced which is a horizontal two-dimensional 'slice' through the body. Dense areas appear lighter and less dense areas darker, as in conventional X-rays. The technique is particularly useful for detecting brain tumours at an early stage.

With the introduction of new techniques, early diagnosis is a rapidly evolving branch of medicine. The journal *New Scientist* is a good source of up-to-date information.

Incubation period

The incubation period is the period of time between original infection and appearance of signs and symptoms. During this period the causative agent is usually multiplying inside the host. Incubation periods vary greatly between diseases. For example, *Salmonella* food poisoning has a characteristically short incubation period of only 12 to 24 hours, whereas measles has a relatively long incubation period of up to 2 weeks. Some viruses may remain dormant in their hosts for several years. The longer the incubation period, the more difficult it becomes to trace close contacts of victims and hence prevent the spread of the disease. A knowledge of the incubation period is vital in determining the length of quarantine (isolation) of contacts.

Infective period

The infective period is the period of time during which a person is capable of passing the disease on to another person. It is often difficult to define this period precisely but special precautions of hygiene should be observed depending on the nature of the disease.

Carriers

A carrier is a person who suffers no signs or symptoms of a disease, but in whom the disease organism can survive to be passed on to another person. Carriers are often important agents in spreading disease because they are very difficult to trace. There are certain diseases such as *Salmonella*, cholera and typhoid in which carriers play a particularly important role in transmission.

Notifiable disease

Some diseases are a serious threat to the community and in most countries doctors and health workers are required to report cases of such diseases to the health authorities. In Britain, the local health authority and the medical officer have legal power to enforce isolation of infected individuals, and to take specimens of blood and urine from suspected contacts. In Britain there are about 20 notifiable diseases, including the more serious childhood diseases (e.g. polio), tuberculosis, pneumonia, puerperal fever and infections transmitted by food or drinking water such as cholera and typhoid. Five epidemic diseases are notifiable to the World Health Organisation in Geneva, namely, cholera, plague, relapsing fever, typhus (not typhoid) and yellow fever.

World Health Organisation

In 1948 the World Health Organisation was set up with its headquarters in Geneva. By 1988 there were 166 member states, who are pledged through the organisation to international cooperation in all aspects of health, including control of disease. Particular emphasis is placed on the prevention of disease.

Some of the diseases of particular concern at present are malaria, tuberculosis, cholera, sexually transmitted diseases (particularly AIDS), leprosy, trachoma (a disease of the eye often leading to blindness), rabies, yaws, bilharziasis, trypanosomiasis, filarial infections and leishmaniasis. In Europe six diseases are subjected to routine immunisation procedures under a WHO programme, namely TB, measles, diphtheria, whooping cough (pertussis), tetanus and polio. All except measles (which has been virtually eradicated) are declining. Diphtheria has declined to the point where it is no longer regarded as a health problem in Europe and polio has been virtually eliminated after a large-scale immunisation campaign (less than 1 in 10 million cases).

Since the early 1970s WHO, in conjunction with other agencies such as the United Nation's Children Fund (UNICEF), has operated an Expanded Programme on Immunisation (EPI) to give protection against the six diseases to children in the developing world. The aim is to give every child protection; at present about 50% receive it.

1.6 Survey of human pathogens

Despite its ideal conditions of temperature, pH, ionic concentration, and nutrient and oxygen availability, relatively few organisms are capable of parasitising the human body. This is because the body has an elaborate system

Table 1.6 Survey of the main groups of organisms containing human pathogens with some common examples of pathogens

RNA viruses	Diseases caused
myxovirus group (Gk. *myxo* – mucus)	influenza A, B and C
paramyxovirus group	measles, mumps
rhabdovirus group (Gk. *rhabdo* – rod)	rabies
picornavirus group (Gk. *pico* – small, *rna* – RNA virus)	poliomyelitis
	common cold (rhinovirus)
	hepatitis A
togavirus group	rubella (German measles)
	yellow fever (an arbovirus; ar–arthropod bo–borne)
	hepatitis B
	lassa fever
rotavirus group	a common cause of infantile gastroenteritis

DNA viruses	Diseases caused
herpes virus group	cold sores (*Herpes simplex*)
	glandular fever or infectious mononucleosis (Epstein-Barr virus)
	chickenpox and shingles (*Varicella zoster* virus or *Herpes zoster*)
adenovirus group	common cause of infection of lymphoid tissue, e.g. tonsils, and infection of upper respiratory tract
poxvirus group	smallpox (no longer in natural environments – only in some research laboratories)

bacteria	Diseases caused
Bordetella pertussis	whooping cough (pertussis)
Streptococcus	sore throats
	scarlet fever
	rheumatic fever
Staphylococcus aureus	septic spots, boils, carbuncles, food poisoning
Corynebacterium diphtheriae	diphtheria
Salmonella – various types	food poisoning (salmonellosis)
Salmonella typhi	typhoid
Salmonella paratyphi	paratyphoid
Shigella	bacillary dysentery
Vibrio cholerae	cholera
Clostridium botulinum	botulism
Clostridium tetani	tetanus (lockjaw)
Mycobacterium tuberculosis	tuberculosis (TB)
Mycobacterium leprae	leprosy
Bacillus anthracis	anthrax
Treponema pallidum	syphilis
Neisseria gonorrhoeae (gonococcus)	gonorrhoea
rickettsia*	
Rickettsia prowazekii	epidemic typhus

chlamydia*

Chlamydia trachomatis	trachoma. Non-specific urethritis (at least 50% of cases). Pelvic inflammatory disease (about 40% of cases)
Chlamydia psittaci	psittacosis

protozoa – unicellular animals**	*Diseases caused*
Plasmodium	malaria
Trichomonas vaginalis	trichomoniasis
Trypanosoma	sleeping sickness
Entamoeba histolytica	amoebic dysentery (amoebiasis)

flatworms	*Diseases caused*
pork tapeworm (*Taenia solium*)	
beef tapeworm (*Taenia saginata*)	
fish tapeworm (*Diphyllobothrium latum*)	
blood fluke (*Schistosoma* species)	schistosomiasis or bilharzia
liver fluke (*Fasciola hepatica*)	fascioliasis

nematode worms (roundworms)	*Diseases caused*
threadworm	
human roundworm (*Ascaris lumbricoides*)	
human hookworm	
threadworm (*Enterobius vermicularis*)	
filarial worm (*Onchocercus volvubis*)	river blindness
filarial worm (*Wuchereria bancrofti*)	filariasis – elephantiasis is a symptom

insects	*Diseases caused*
head louse (*Pediculosis capitis*)	
body louse (*Pediculosis corporis*)	
crab louse (pubic louse) (*Phthirus pubis*)	*Lice are also important vectors of disease, e.g. typhus*

arachnids	*Diseases caused*
mite (*Sarcoptes scabiei*)	scabies
	Mites may act as vectors of certain diseases, e.g. scrub typhus

fungi	*Diseases caused*
Microsporum and *Trichophyton*	ringworm of the scalp (tinea) and ringworm of the feet (athlete's foot)
	ringworm of the body or groin
Candida albicans (a yeast)	candidiasis (oral thrush or vaginal thrush (vaginitis))

*Organisms intermediate in size between viruses and bacteria. Like viruses, they can multiply only inside living cells.

**It is now recommended that the Protozoa are classified in the Kingdom Protoctista, not the animal kingdom.

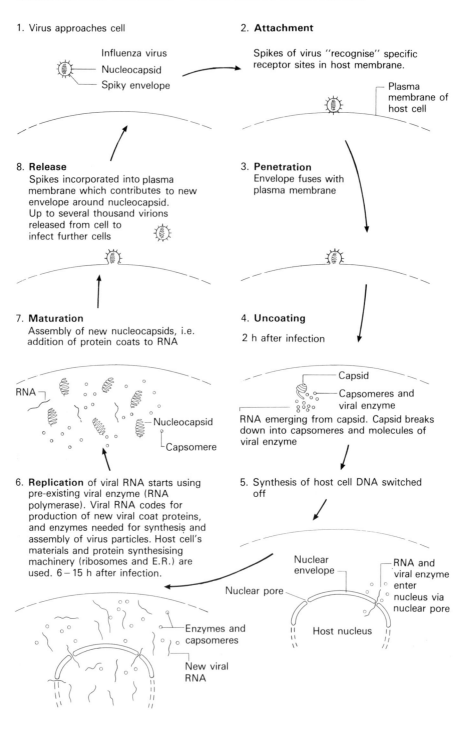

1. Virus approaches cell

Influenza virus
— Nucleocapsid
— Spiky envelope

2. **Attachment**

Spikes of virus "recognise" specific receptor sites in host membrane.

— Plasma membrane of host cell

8. **Release**
Spikes incorporated into plasma membrane which contributes to new envelope around nucleocapsid. Up to several thousand virions released from cell to infect further cells

3. **Penetration**
Envelope fuses with plasma membrane

7. **Maturation**
Assembly of new nucleocapsids, i.e. addition of protein coats to RNA

4. **Uncoating**

2 h after infection

RNA ┐
— Nucleocapsid
└Capsomere

— Capsid
—Capsomeres and viral enzyme

RNA emerging from capsid. Capsid breaks down into capsomeres and molecules of viral enzyme

6. **Replication** of viral RNA starts using pre-existing viral enzyme (RNA polymerase). Viral RNA codes for production of new viral coat proteins, and enzymes needed for synthesis and assembly of virus particles. Host cell's materials and protein synthesising machinery (ribosomes and E.R.) are used. 6 – 15 h after infection.

5. Synthesis of host cell DNA switched off

Nuclear envelope
Nuclear pore

—RNA and viral enzyme enter nucleus via nuclear pore

—Enzymes and capsomeres

Host nucleus

New viral RNA

Figure 1.3 Life cycle of an influenza virus. Note: capsid = protective coat made of protein subunits called capsomeres

of defences, including the immune system which is discussed in chapter 5. Nevertheless, certain organisms from a wide range of groups, as shown in table 1.6, have developed the extreme specialisation needed to penetrate these defences. By living and growing inside, or sometimes on the surface, of the body, these organisms sometimes cause disease. A disease-causing organism is called a **pathogen**, and is described as **pathogenic**. As table 1.6 illustrates, the greatest range of diseases is caused by viruses and bacteria. The study of viruses and bacteria, together with fungi, forms the branch of biology known as **microbiology**. The organisms are called **microbes**, or **microorganisms**, because they can be clearly seen only if a microscope is used. The structure of viruses and bacteria, and bacterial reproduction, are dealt with in most standard 'A' level biology textbooks.

Viruses

The life cycle of the influenza virus, an RNA virus, is illustrated in fig. 1.3. Details of life cycles vary between viruses but the main phases are similar. The host cell usually dies as a result of the infection, but in a few exceptional cases, as with certain cancer-inducing viruses and with the AIDS virus (HIV), viral DNA can become integrated into the host DNA where it may remain dormant.

A summary of the main characteristics of viruses and how they differ from other organisms is given below.

1 Viruses are the smallest living organisms. Size ranges from about 20 nm to 300 nm. For comparison, the sharp point of a pin is about 50 000 nm in diameter. The average bacterial cell is about 1000 nm and the average animal cell about 20 000 nm in diameter. The maximum resolution of a light microscope is about 170 nm. (1000 nm = 1 μm, 1000 μm = 1 mm, 1000 mm = 1 m)

2 Viruses have a very simple structure. They consist of one molecule of a nucleic acid surrounded by a protective coat called the **capsid**. The capsid is made up of many protein subunits called **capsomeres**. The whole particle is called a **virion**. All other organisms have a cellular structure, each cell being surrounded by a plasma membrane containing cytoplasm with organelles. Viruses have no cytoplasm or organelles of their own.

3 The genetic material (nucleic acid) of the virus is either DNA or RNA. In other organisms the genetic material is always DNA.

4 All viruses are parasites and cannot reproduce outside the host cells. This point is the key to understanding viruses. They can escape from cells and be transmitted from one cell to another but cannot function until they are back in a cell environment and can take over the cell machinery of the host. This they do for the sole purpose of reproduction.

2   Some infectious diseases caused by viruses and bacteria

2.1   Influenza (flu)

Good example of: droplet infection (airborne); a disease that overcomes resistance by producing new strains (new antigens).

Causative agent and background to the disease

Influenza is caused by an RNA virus of the **myxovirus** group (see fig. 1.3 for life cycle). The virus has a spiky envelope. The spikes consist of two types of antigen which interact specifically with the host cell.

There are three forms of the virus, influenza A, B and C. Influenza A is responsible for major epidemics and pandemics. An **epidemic** is said to occur when a disease spreads rapidly through a large number of people. When epidemics spread across whole continents they are called **pandemics**, for example, the disastrous pandemic of 1918–19, which caused about 20 million deaths worldwide, including 150 000 in Britain. Further flu pandemics occurred in 1946 and 1957 (Asian flu) and 1968 and 1969 (Hong Kong flu). Deaths are mainly from secondary respiratory infections by bacteria causing bronchitis and pneumonia. Influenza B usually causes a milder and more local outbreak of the disease. Influenza C is uncommon and causes only minor respiratory illness similar to the common cold.

New variants of the viruses appear from time to time when one of the two surface antigens mentioned above changes. New antigens correspond with the appearance of new pandemics. The lack of resistance to new variants is due to the fact that the body's immune system has never previously been exposed to the new antigens (see chapter 5). The virus causes infection before the body has time to build up antibodies to the disease.

Transmission

Influenza is highly infectious and transmission is by **droplet infection**. The virus affects the respiratory passages, particularly of the nose and throat. Droplets of mucus and saliva carrying virus particles are released during coughing, sneezing, talking and normal breathing. They may be inhaled directly by others, or evaporate, leaving airborne virus particles that can survive dry conditions for some time. Transmission is more likely in crowded places and in poorly ventilated rooms.

Signs and symptoms

The incubation period is 1 to 3 days. The earliest signs are fever, with a sudden rise in temperature to as high as 39°C (about 102°F) and shivering. The earliest symptoms are aching limbs and back, headache, sore throat and a dry cough.

Later, the cough becomes looser and a runny nose develops. Weakness, lack of energy and sometimes depression accompany recovery, which usually takes from 1 to 2 weeks.

Complications

In rare cases, notably in very young children or elderly people, the infection may spread from the upper respiratory tract down the trachea to the lungs. Acute bronchitis or pneumonia (secondary infection of the lungs by certain bacteria) may occur. A combination of bronchitis and pneumonia is termed bronchopneumonia, which may be fatal.

Control – treatment and prevention

As explained previously, control of diseases requires both treatment of existing cases and measures to try to prevent further cases.

Treatment There is little that can be done to treat viral diseases on a large scale, since the generally available antibiotics do not kill viruses. Signs and symptoms may be treated. For example, aspirin may be taken by adults and children over 12 years of age for aches and fever. If secondary bacterial infection occurs or is likely, antibiotics may be taken to kill the bacteria. Rest in bed, and frequent drinking of water, is advised, at least until the temperature returns to normal.

Prevention Standard hygiene includes use of handkerchiefs or tissues, and ventilation of rooms. Anti-influenza vaccines can be prepared, but are effective only against existing strains of the virus. Those most at risk from influenza, such as football teams, the elderly, diabetics and medical staff are advised to have annual injections in the autumn.

The vaccine contains **dead** viruses of current A and B strains. The viruses are first cultured in a fertilised chicken's egg. Virus particles obtained from throat washings of infected patients are injected into fluid-filled cavities associated with the growing chick, such as the amniotic cavity, and large numbers of viruses grow in the cells lining the cavities. After incubation, fluid containing viruses is removed, the viruses are killed with formalin or ultra-violet radiation and purified. Protection cannot be guaranteed and is short-lived, so mass vaccination is not recommended.

Every time a new strain appears, new vaccines have to be prepared. Early warning systems for new outbreaks have been set up. The World Health Organisation monitors epidemic influenza and runs the World Influenza Centre in London. This centre, together with another in the U.S.A., is responsible for collecting and identifying current strains of the virus and if necessary sending samples to laboratories around the world for preparation of vaccines. General practitioners may also report suspected new outbreaks. Attempts are being made to develop a live vaccine.

Social implications

Epidemics of influenza have important social implications because they result in massive rises in sick leave with a consequent loss of working hours, and strain on the health services. Also, each new epidemic is accompanied by a relatively high death toll.

2.2 Poliomyelitis (polio)

Good example of: effectiveness of vaccination in preventing disease. Infection is airborne (droplet) and faecal-borne.

Causative agent and background to the disease

Polio is caused by an RNA virus. It exists in 3 strains, 1, 2 and 3. Type 1 is the most virulent. In highly developed countries the disease tends to occur in epidemics rather than being widespread and endemic as in many developing countries (an **endemic disease** is one which is present at a low level all the time in the population).

Although there was a major epidemic of polio in the U.S.A. in 1916, with 6000 deaths and 27 000 left paralysed, epidemics did not occur in Britain until 1947. In the summer of 1947 700 deaths occurred, and summer epidemics recurred in subsequent years, not only in Britain but in other highly developed areas like Scandinavia. The disease therefore came to be a dreaded one in the early 1950s, and concerted efforts were made to develop reliable vaccines (see *Prevention*).

It is thought likely that before 1947 in Britain, and currently in developing countries where the disease is endemic, infection may have been so widespread that it commonly occurred in infancy when there is still some protection from maternal antibodies, and that natural immunity therefore existed in a large proportion of the population. Isolated epidemics tend to occur only when general standards of hygiene have improved above a certain level.

Transmission

The virus multiplies mainly in the gut after entering through the mouth or nose (see Signs and symptoms). Viruses therefore leave the body in the faeces and faecal contamination is a common means of transmission. There are various means by which traces of faecal material may be passed on to another individual. Unless there is proper sewage disposal, faeces are commonly deposited in or near water, such as rivers, which is used for drinking. Food may become contaminated by washing it in water containing faecal material, or by touching it with unwashed hands, or when vectors such as flies walk on it. Finally, contamination of objects such as door handles may result in hand to mouth transfer of faecal material.

A second major method of transmission is droplet infection (see Transmission of influenza) since the virus multiplies in the nose and pharynx in the acute phase of the disease.

Signs and symptoms

The virus enters the body by way of the mouth or nose, infects the intestines and then spreads to the blood. The incubation period is usually 1 to 2 weeks. Early signs and symptoms are severe headaches, sore throat, fever and vomiting followed by pain in the neck and back muscles. This is due to irritation of the meninges, the membranes that surround the brain and spinal cord. In most cases the disease is a relatively minor one, subsiding after a few days. However, in severe cases, the virus may attack motor neurones in the spinal cord and hindbrain. Temporary paralysis may occur and it may take several years for complete recovery. In a few cases recovery is incomplete and paralysis may be permanent. The paralysis normally affects the legs and to a lesser extent the arms. If the brain is affected paralysis of the muscles involved in swallowing or breathing may occur. The latter is the usual cause of death and necessitates use of an artificial breathing machine for survival. Children are the most likely to suffer.

Control – treatment and prevention

Treatment If paralysis occurs, patients are monitored closely for signs of respiratory weakness. In cases of respiratory failure the patient must be connected to an artificial respiration machine (ventilator). When the illness subsides they are given physiotherapy to aid recovery.

Prevention Proper sewage disposal is essential (see also *Salmonella* and cholera). Infected persons are kept in isolation, usually in hospital, for at least 3 weeks. Their contacts are also quarantined for 3 weeks, the maximum incubation period.

The disease is **notifiable** (see section 1.5). It is usual in the case of polio to vaccinate immediately all possible contacts. Polio outbreaks are also monitored by the World Health Organisation so that international exchange of information occurs.

Attempts to produce a safe polio vaccine have a long history. Epidemics in this country were brought under control by use of the Salk vaccine developed by Jonas Salk in the U.S.A. and introduced into Britain in 1956. It contained **killed** virus, and reduced the incidence of paralytic polio among treated children to about one quarter that of untreated children. In 1962 however, an improved vaccine was introduced, the Sabin vaccine. This contained **living** attenuated viruses of the 3 strains. An **attenuated** organism is one which has been rendered harmless by some chemical or heat treatment (see section 5.7). It was administered orally (by mouth) rather than being injected, which made treatment both easier and painless and therefore more attractive. Supplied as 3 drops on a sugar lump it could even be pleasant! In addition it gave better protection than the Salk vaccine. The vaccine is extremely safe, with only one case of paralysis being caused per several million vaccinations. The result has been to eradicate polio almost completely in those countries like Britain which have adopted mass vaccination programmes (compare diphtheria). For example, in Britain there have been no deaths from paralytic polio since 1966. In 1980 only 3 cases were notified. In 1961, the year before oral vaccines were introduced, there were 707 notified cases of paralytic polio in England and Wales and 59 deaths.

The recommended vaccine programme is shown in table 5.2. Continued control requires an infant immunisation rate of 80 to 90%.

Vaccination or booster doses may be recommended for people who are planning to travel abroad to areas where polio is endemic.

As with other diseases that have been brought under control there is a need for maintained vigilance and continuation of the vaccination programme. The disease could be reintroduced at any time from countries where it is endemic. Also, a change in the attenuated virus, which lives permanently in our guts, might result in increased virulence. It can also be argued that there is now more risk of acquiring paralytic polio from a vaccination than from natural sources, which has led to consideration of using safer killed vaccines now that control has been established.

2.3   Salmonella food poisoning (salmonellosis)
Good example of: food-borne and faecal-borne disease.

Causative agent and background to the disease
The *Salmonella* group of bacteria is very large and contains many pathogens that infect the guts of animals, including humans (see table 1.6). Food poisoning (salmonellosis) is caused by a variety of *Salmonella* organisms and is a classic food-borne disease.

Food poisoning is a term used to describe a disease in which there is a rapid onset of diarrhoea and, usually, vomiting after eating contaminated food. The cause may vary, however. Certain bacteria and viruses can cause food poisoning by infecting the gut, and sometimes the toxic products of bacteria may accumulate in food before consumption, as with staphylococcal food poisoning. **Gastroenteritis**, which is usually caused by viruses, and **dysentery**, which may be amoebic or bacterial in origin, are further diseases which may be confused with true food poisoning. In the case of dysentery, symptoms are severe enough for early diagnosis to be straightforward. In Britain, about 90% of reported cases of food poisoning are due to *Salmonella* or staphylococcal infection. In this book, we shall consider only *Salmonella* food poisoning.

Transmission
Since salmonellosis affects other animals as well as humans, it is classically transmitted to humans when they eat the products of infected food animals, such as poultry, pigs, cattle (meat or milk) and horses. It is therefore classically regarded as a **food-borne disease**. The faeces of domestic pets and of pests such as rats and mice may also contaminate human food. An important point to realise is that modern methods of large-scale food production have led to a large reservoir of salmonella organisms which cycle regularly through various well established routes, some of which are summarised in fig. 2.1.

The faeces of infected people are highly infectious and may continue to be so for months. Human **carriers** (infected people who show no signs or symptoms) are an important risk. They may pass infected faeces intermittently or continuously over many years (see Control). There is a risk of build-up of *Salmonella* in abbatoirs, butchers' shops, in factories and on farms, especially where intensive or factory farming is practised, as with battery hens. Outbreaks of epidemic proportions among animals are extremely serious in the latter situations and strenuous efforts are made to avoid them.

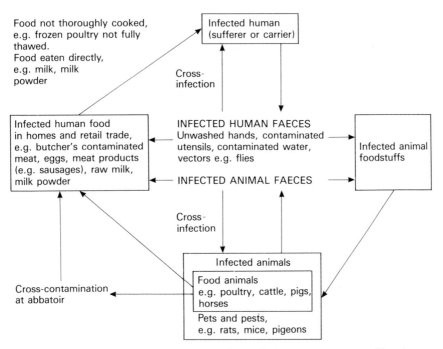

Figure 2.1 The *Salmonella* cycle; major routes only are shown. Note importance of faecal contamination; cross-contamination and cross-infection are increased by poor hygiene

The inadequate thawing of frozen poultry is one of the commonest causes of the disease.

Background levels of *Salmonella* are extremely hard to remove. In 1986 a Farley's factory producing milk powder for babies had to be closed once *Salmonella* contamination of the powder had been discovered. The factory was sold to Boots who were unable to get rid of all traces of contamination with the result that a new factory had to be built. The source of contamination was never clearly established but was thought unlikely to be the milk itself. Traces of contaminated faecal material from pigeons nesting in the roof may have got into air inlets through which the air used to dry the milk was taken. However, this is purely speculation. Nevertheless, it serves to illustrate the important commercial implications of food-borne disease, and the difficulties it imposes on the food industry.

Signs and symptoms

The incubation period is characteristically short, usually about 12 to 24 hours. Signs and symptoms appear suddenly. The main sign is diarrhoea accompanied by vomiting and usually fever. Symptoms of abdominal pain or discomfort, and usually headache occur. In extreme cases dehydration may be severe and require treatment (see below). Most people suffer relatively mild symptoms and recover within a few days.

Complications may occur. Dehydration can lead to death through clinical shock, low blood pressure and renal failure, especially in the elderly or very young, particularly babies. Rarely the bacteria spread into the blood and thus to other organs. Death may result from septicaemia ('blood poisoning').

Control – treatment and prevention

Treatment Rest in bed at home with an adequate fluid intake is generally advised. If severe dehydration occurs, hospitalisation is recommended so that the correct balance of fluid and salt can be restored. Antibiotics are only recommended in severe cases, particularly when septicaemia sets in. Recently more drug-resistant and virulent *Salmonella* strains have begun to appear which pose a potentially greater threat.

Prevention Figure 2.1 shows many points at which obvious preventive measures can be taken. Many of the measures are standard for diseases involving transmission by faecal material:

1 **Proper sewage disposal**
2 **Meat inspection** by an environmental health officer. Ill animals can be identified and not used, but it is difficult or impossible to identify carriers. There is no compulsory inspection of poultry, but any outbreak of salmonellosis on a farm would be dealt with immediately.
3 **Hygiene in the food trade** Environmental health officers regularly inspect shops, restaurants, kitchens and factories. Food must be protected from rodents and where possible from flies. Butchers in particular must try to reduce the risk of cross-contamination between meat by regularly cleaning utensils and work surfaces, particularly chopping boards. It is important that raw and cooked meats are stored and handled separately.
4 **Hygiene in the home** Storage, preparation and cooking of food are the three key areas. Raw meat should not be tasted or allowed to contaminate other food. It should be stored in a cool place or refrigerated to minimise bacterial growth. Surfaces and utensils must be kept clean. The most important measure required is *thorough cooking of foods* because it is almost inevitable that contaminated meat, particularly poultry, will occasionally be purchased. Up to 10% of sausages may contain *Salmonella* bacteria, for example. High temperatures kill the bacteria. The greatest danger is not thawing frozen poultry sufficiently. Recommended thawing times are given on the wrappers of such birds and should be observed. A large turkey, for example, may take 48 hours to thaw properly at room temperature.
5 **Control of flies** Flies act as vectors of the disease by transferring faecal material to food.
5 **Control of rodents** Faecal material from rodents may contaminate stored food.
7 **Personal hygiene** Anyone who has contracted the disease should observe very strict personal hygiene for as long as live *Salmonella* bacteria can be isolated from the faeces. This requires regular checking by a doctor. It is particularly important to wash the hands after using the toilet.

8 **Purification of water** This is not as critical as with water-borne diseases.

Salmonellosis is a notifiable disease, and people who have had the disease are legally prevented from working in the food industry until their faeces have been proven to be free from the bacteria. Carriers are similarly usually prevented from working in the food industry unless under strictly controlled circumstances, and are entitled to full pay if no alternative employment can be found.

2.4 Cholera

Good example of: water-borne disease, faecal-borne disease, importance of water purification, genetically engineered vaccine.

Causative agent

Cholera is caused by the bacterium *Vibrio cholerae*. The disease is endemic in parts of Asia, particularly India. Occasional epidemics break out in other countries. It kills millions of people in Bangladesh, India, Pakistan, Sri Lanka and Africa every year.

Transmission

Cholera is a disease of the gut and, as with typhoid, which is also a good example of a water-borne and faecal-borne bacterial disease, transmission starts with infected faeces.

Both cholera and typhoid are primarily water-borne diseases, with epidemic outbreaks occuring if drinking water is contaminated. Faeces are most commonly introduced directly into water by defaecation, but leaking sewers or poorly sited pit latrines may contaminate ground water, wells, reservoirs or rivers. Drinking such water, or washing food in it, is a common source of infection in developing countries. Both diseases may also be spread by contamination of food with human faeces as with *Salmonella* (see fig. 2.1). Symptomless carriers are important agents in spreading the disease.

Signs and symptoms

The incubation period is from several hours to 5 days. The chief sign is a rapid onset of severe diarrhoea due to production of a bacterial toxin in the gut. Abdominal pain and vomiting may also occur. Fever is absent. In severe cases diarrhoea is passed almost continuously and its murky appearance has led to its being called 'rice water'. Dehydration and loss of vital body salts is rapid and can lead to death within 24 hours. Up to 15 litres of fluid (25 pints) may be lost per day. Leg cramp, clinical shock and acute renal failure also occur. Mild or symptomless cases are also common.

Control – treatment and prevention

Treatment The disease may be treated with the antibiotic tetracycline, but recently tetracycline-resistant strains have appeared in Bangladesh. Fluids, glucose and salts must be replaced, usually orally.

Prevention Cholera is a notifiable disease in Britain and outbreaks anywhere must also be notified to the World Health Organisation. Like typhoid and paratyphoid, the two most important preventive measures are proper sewage treatment and purification of water supplies. Control of flies is important, as is personal hygiene, particularly in handling food. Patients should be isolated and particular care taken that faeces and vomit, both of which contain millions of vibrios, are disposed of hygienically. Close contacts should be treated with tetracycline, and other people in the area may be vaccinated. The cholera vaccine contains heat-killed bacteria and is not very effective, giving partial protection for up to 6 months. Development of a genetically engineered vaccine is underway, however, which promises to give lifelong protection (see 5.7).

Restrictions on travel from infected areas and quarantine of visitors from these areas is also an effective preventive measure.

2.5   Tuberculosis (TB)
Good example of: role of social factors in disease, safe vaccination.

Causative agent and background to the disease
Tuberculosis is caused by the bacterium *Mycobacterium tuberculosis*. It is most commonly a chronic disease, that is, a disease which persists for a long period of time but with undramatic symptoms that may not be disabling. The most common form is **pulmonary TB**, which affects the lungs, but many other organs may be affected, such as the liver, lymph nodes, brain, kidney, genital organs and bones.

There are two main strains of the bacterium, the **human** and **bovine** forms, the latter of which affects cattle but can be passed on to humans.

Worldwide, TB is a very important disease with an estimated one to two million deaths per year. The cost of implementing large-scale vaccination programmes is a major difficulty. In Britain, although the disease has declined dramatically (annual notifications numbered over 40 000 per year in the 1930s and 1940s) there are still around 6000 notifications per year and it is on the increase in immigrant communities.

Transmission
Transmission is by droplet infection (see section 2.1) although less commonly may be by direct physical contact (**contagion**). Exposure to risk must usually occur over a prolonged period. It is therefore typically associated with over-crowded living conditions, particularly if an infected person is sleeping in the same room as others.

Bovine TB affects cattle and can be passed into their milk. Worldwide, milk is another important source of the disease, but in Britain this is no longer the case for two reasons. Firstly, all cattle are regularly checked for TB and are slaughtered if infected. Secondly, milk is normally pasteurised, a process which kills the bacteria.

Signs and symptoms
With pulmonary TB there are characteristically two phases. The first (**primary**) phase lasts for several months during which small local infections may occur in various parts of the body such as the lungs, and a dry cough may be experi-

enced. This phase may pass unnoticed, although chest X-rays show where infection has occurred, and the tuberculin test is positive (see Prevention). Some bacteria may remain dormant for several years and become active later in old age or when health is poor. This **secondary phase** is known as **consumption**, and mainly affects the lungs. Coughing up of sputum and sometimes of blood occurs. The course of the disease from here is very variable. Asian immigrants, Scots and Irish tend to have poor natural resistance to the disease.

Control – treatment and prevention

Treatment The disease is treated by a combination of antibiotics over a period of 9–12 months.

Prevention Tuberculosis is a notifiable disease and contacts of infected patients are traced. Any contact over the age of 15 years is X-rayed, as are children under 15 who react positively to the tuberculin test (see below). Other children are vaccinated (see below). Routine mass X-rays of the community are no longer performed, but health visitors may recommend X-rays in areas or situations of high risk. Sputum must be disposed of hygienically. Infected or recovered persons should not work in the food industry or with children under the age of 12. Teachers must have X-rays before entering training for the profession. Relapses are possible and favoured by poor social conditions. There is a strong social element in disease prevention. Overcrowded living conditions favour spread of the disease. Immediate rehousing is necessary if an infected person cannot sleep in a separate bedroom. Poverty, inadequate diet and social class are all correlated with development of the disease. In Britain, it is now most common among the elderly. Patients are isolated during the brief infectious phase of the disease.

The vaccine used contains live, chemically attenuated bacteria, and is called the **BCG** vaccine (Bacille Calmette Guerin, the latter two names being those of the two French scientists who developed the vaccine). It is probably the safest vaccine currently in use. It is recommended that it be administered to schoolchildren at the age of 10–13 years. They are first tuberculin tested, which establishes whether natural immunity has already been obtained by previous infection. An extract from tubercle bacteria, called **tuberculin**, is smeared on to the skin and an instrument called a **Heaf gun**, with a ring of short needles, is used to introduce it just below the skin. A ring of small red swellings, reaching a maximum after 3 days, indicates a positive response and existing immunity. About 8% of British school-children are tuberculin-positive. If the reaction is sufficiently positive, they may be recommended to have X-rays to check that the disease is not active. Tuberculin-negative children are injected with the vaccine, also with a Heaf gun. A characteristic lesion persists for several weeks and may leave a small scar. Vaccination may be given at birth if there is a greater than average risk, as in families where TB is already present, or in Asian immigrant families. The BCG vaccine gives long-term protection and has resulted in a dramatic reduction in cases of TB in the post-war period in Britain. However, this should be seen in the perspective of long-term decline due to changing social conditions (see fig. 1.2 (c) and section 1.3). Prevention of **bovine tuberculosis** has been discussed under Transmission.

3   Sexually transmitted diseases

3.1   Introduction

The sexually transmitted diseases embrace a wide variety of diseases of varying severity. They were formerly known as venereal diseases (VD) and after the First World War, a network of special VD clinics was set up in Britain which offered free advice and treatment. This was an excellent initiative, but unfortunately there tended to be a social stigma attached to the term VD and attendance at the clinics was often prejudiced as a result. There was both a sense of fear and mystery associated with the subject, and it was rarely openly discussed. The social revolution which has occurred in post-Second World War Britain has included a sexual revolution in which attitudes to sex have changed markedly. In line with the more enlightened attitudes towards sexual problems in general, the term VD was dropped and substituted by STD or sexually transmitted diseases. Even more recently, use of the terms **genito-urinary infection** and **genito-urinary clinics** and **genito-urinary medicine (GUM)** have become common.

As will be shown, changes in the incidence of STDs in society seem to be correlated with changing attitudes to sex. Hence, as with other diseases, there is an important social dimension to the diseases. It is useful to look at the incidence of two of the most common STDs, gonorrhoea and syphilis, for which good records have been kept in Britain for a long period.

Figure 3.1 shows the incidence of these diseases since 1925. It can be seen that the trends are markedly different. Overall incidence of STDs increased during and immediately following the Second World War, but overall there has been a spectacular decline in syphilis since 1925, whereas gonorrhoea declined from 1925 to the mid 1950s, rose to even greater heights after that, and has only recently started falling again. The rise from the 1950s was particularly marked among women. Compared with other infections such as those studied in chapter 2 this is an unusual phenomenon. A closer inspection of the syphilis figures also reveals a rise in new cases in the 1970s, especially among men. This, however, was due mainly to a rise in the incidence of the disease among homosexuals, a reflection of the greater liberation enjoyed within the homosexual community. Syphilis is ten times more prevalent among homosexual men than heterosexual men. Gonorrhoea is three times more prevalent. Reasons for the higher incidence of these diseases among homosexuals are not clear. The impact of AIDS (section 3.9) is changing sexual behaviour again and figures for STDs are beginning to reflect this, with falls during the 1980s being recorded for gonorrhoea and syphilis (fig. 3.1). New cases of syphilis and gonorrhoea in England and Wales fell by 20% and 12% respectively in 1986, and by 25% and a dramatic 40% respectively in 1987, mainly among males although also among females.

Another interesting statistic is the number of new cases of gonorrhoea in girls under 16. Since the mid 1960s these have been increasing at about the same rate, possibly slightly faster, than those for older age groups and have only started a downturn from 1984. There are roughly three times as many cases of gonorrhoea among girls under 16 than among boys under 16 and it is also more common in girls than boys in the 16 to 19 age group.

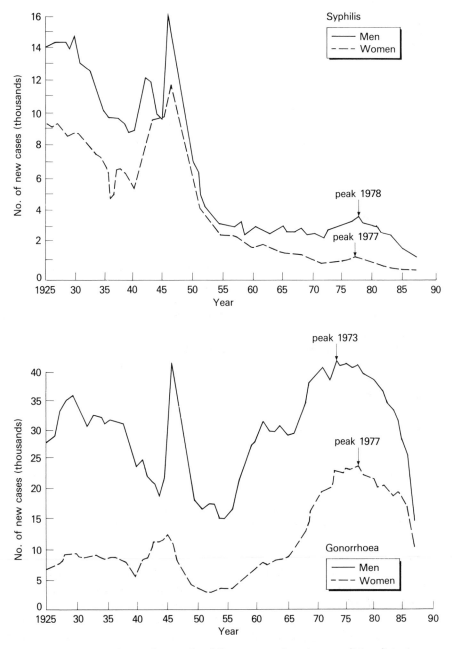

Figure 3.1 New cases of gonorrhoea and syphilis seen at genito-urinary medicine clinics in Britain in the period 1925 to 1987, from *Lecture notes on sexually transmitted diseases*, R. Nicol Thin, Blackwell Scientific Publications Ltd. (1982)

There are a variety of factors that could contribute to this trend, both biological and social. For example, has there been a change in the effectiveness of antibiotics, making it more difficult to cure gonorrhoea? Have methods of gathering information become more efficient or has diagnosis become more reliable? What is the true extent of the increase in sexual promiscuity? How can we account for a difference in the pattern of gonorrhoea and syphilis, and what about STDs? Is there insufficient education among those at risk or has improved education resulted in more people attending clinics, thus boosting recorded cases? Answers will be given to some of these questions, others are more debatable.

Gonorrhoea and syphilis were the two STDs which attracted most attention until recently, but they comprise only about 10% of the cases of STD treated in clinics today. Overall there has been a three-fold rise in recorded cases of STDs in Britain since the mid 1970s, with diseases other than gonorrhoea and syphilis coming into prominence (see fig. 3.2). However the number of new cases (over 600 000) in 1987 decreased by 4% compared with 1986, the first

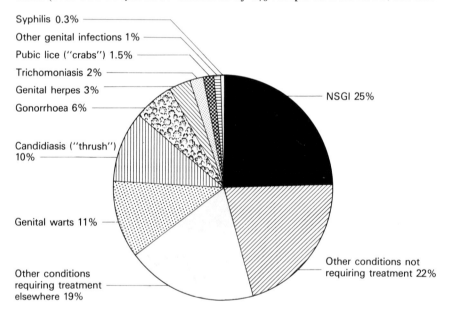

Figure 3.2 New cases seen at National Health Service Genito-Urinary Medicine clinics in England and Wales, 1986 (DHSS)

fall in the number of cases since 1962. Since the 1970s there has been an increase in the viral diseases herpes, hepatitis and genital warts (the latter associated with a higher incidence of cervical cancer). AIDS (acquired immune deficiency syndrome) is a 'new' viral disease. *Chlamydia* has come to be recognised as the most common STD in Britain. Other common diseases on the increase until 1987 are non-specific genital infections, candidiasis (see fig. 3.3), trichomoniasis (14 261 new cases in England and Wales 1986) and pubic lice (pediculosis) (9657 new cases). Details of these diseases are given in this chapter. In reading about the individual diseases, the reader should try to

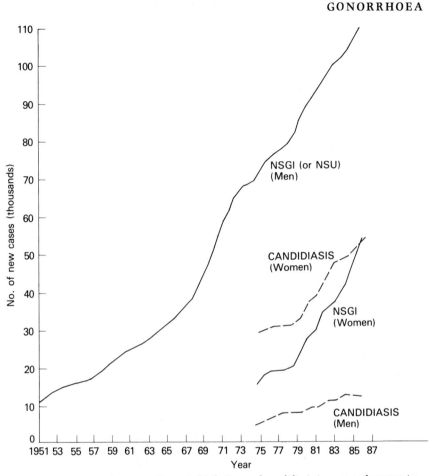

Figure 3.3 New cases of non-specific genital infection and candidiasis in men and women in England and Wales for the period 1975 to 1986. Additional statistics for NSGI in men from 1951 to 1974 are given (DHSS)

retain an overall picture of the whole spectrum of STDs, their social consequences and implications and the strategies which must be adopted in tackling this class of disease.

3.2 Gonorrhoea

Causative agent and background to the disease

The incidence of gonorrhoea in Britain has already been noted (fig. 3.1). Worldwide there has been an increasing trend with over 60 million new cases being *reported* each year in the 1970s (probably more than 200 million *actual* new cases). Since up to 10% of cases in men and 50% of cases in women present no symptoms many cases probably go unreported and statistics are therefore of low reliability. Gonorrhoea, commonly known as the 'clap', is caused by the bacterium *Neisseria gonorrhoeae*, or gonococcus. Typically the organism infects the epithelium of the lower part of the urethra in men, and the cervix and urethra in women. The urethra is the urinary passage and infection of this is called **urethritis**. The latter is termed gonococcal urethritis when gonococcus is established as the cause. Infection of the rectum is possible in homosexual or bisexual men and in some cases the rectum of women may be affected even if anal sex has not occurred. Gonorrhoea can affect the throat in cases of oral sex. The conjunctiva of newborn babies can become infected during birth if the mother is infected.

Signs and symptoms

The incubation period is usually about 5 days, though it varies from 2–10 days. The first symptom noticeable in the male is a burning discomfort on passing urine. Later, there may be a slight discharge of yellow pus from the tip of the penis. Other possible signs and symptoms include fever, headache and general malaise. If untreated, complications may arise. The infection may spread up the urethra to other parts of the reproductive system such as the Cowper's gland and epididymis, causing swelling and abscesses. Constriction of the urethra as scar tissue builds up is possible, but rare. This makes urination and ejaculation painful. A form of arthritis and spots on the skin more commonly occur in women than men.

In up to half of women there are no signs or symptoms at all, and the disease may be detected only as a result of diagnosis of a male partner. There may be a change in the nature and quantity of the vaginal discharge and some discomfort, as in the male, on urinating. There may be slight headaches and fever which might easily pass unnoticed. Untreated, the infection may spread from the cervix through the uterus and into the Fallopian tubes where pus may accumulate. If the tubes become blocked, the woman is rendered sterile since ova cannot pass to the uterus. It is estimated that up to 2000 women a year become sterile as a result of gonnorrhoea.

Control – treatment and prevention

Treatment Fortunately, gonococcus has proved to be very sensitive to penicillin, although its sensitivity has gradually decreased. One oral dose is usually sufficient to cure the disease. Penicillin has the added advantage of being cheap and safe. In parts of the world where penicillin is freely available, as in Africa and the Far East, gonococcus is more resistant. In 1976, the first totally penicillin-resistant strain of the bacterium was reported in Africa and the Far East. This contained a gene coding for the enzyme penicillinase, which breaks down penicillin. The strain had spread to Europe by 1979. At present in Britain about 25% of isolated gonococci show *partial* resistance to penicillin and the number of cases involving totally resistant strains is increasing. Other drugs must be used if the patient is allergic to penicillin. Effectiveness of the treatment is normally checked by 3 further visits to the doctor over a 2 week period.

Prevention Prevention of all STDs depends upon the same basic principles. These are:

    1 **Sexual abstinence** The obvious way to avoid sexually transmitted disease is to avoid sexual intercourse. The more sexually promiscuous a person is, the greater the risk to which they are exposed. The enormous rise in gonorrhoea cases since the 1950s (see fig. 3.1) is

thought to be attributable mainly to increased sexual freedom and promiscuity. The introduction of the Pill in the 1960s as a contraceptive which offered 100% protection if correctly used, was undoubtedly a spur to this freedom since it removed one of the greatest barriers to promiscuity, namely the risk of an unwanted pregnancy. However, to blame the rise solely on the Pill is clearly too superficial an analysis. Gonorrhoea, and promiscuity, were increasing before its introduction. Also an increase in promiscuity independent of the Pill is indicated by the increasing abortion rate and the number of unwanted pregnancies. Following the Second World War there was a changing moral climate and changing social conditions. A new generation was rejecting old values that had been seen to fail in many cases and there was the spectacular emergence of youth culture, with greater freedom and economic independence.

Moral arguments can become very confused. For example, is it morally sound to argue that sexual intercourse is wrong because of the risk of contracting disease? What is obviously important is that everyone understands the risks as clearly as possible. Each year in Britain about 1 person in 1000 visits a clinic to be treated for gonorrhoea. Two-thirds are male and it is more common on a percentage basis in those with several sexual partners. People who enter into stable, long-term relationships, whether within or outside marriage, are clearly at less risk.

2 **Tracing of contacts** In order to reduce the spread of STDs the importance of tracing sexual contacts must be clearly understood. The patient is largely responsible for this. The patient must try to identify the person from whom they caught the disease as well as anyone they may have infected. This is particularly important with gonorrhoea because the woman may not develop the symptoms, and may only be alerted by an infected male partner. Tracing the partner may be difficult if casual relationships are entered into.

3 **Effective diagnosis, treatment and follow-up** In the first instance, accurate diagnosis is essential. In the case of gonorrhoea, the vagueness of the signs and symptoms (or absence in many women) means that the disease often goes unnoticed and is difficult to diagnose. Diagnosis can only be confirmed by isolation of gonococci from infected tissue. This is probably one of the main reasons why gonorrhoea is increasing so rapidly compared with syphilis, where diagnosis is easy. Once a diagnosis has been made treatment may be given, but follow-up visits to clinics, together with abstention from sexual intercourse, are essential until recovery is complete.

4 **Education** A basic knowledge of the facts concerning STDs is obviously a very important factor in their prevention. In Britain, sex education generally is a compulsory part of the secondary school curriculum. Further information is widely available, for example from the Health Education Authority, local health visitors, GPs and the media. Education in the social as well as the biological sphere is important. Sex

continues to remain an emotive and to some extent taboo subject in our society. A common attitude relating to STDs, for example, is that of moral retribution, the feeling that people get what they deserve. This can even undermine the funding of this important branch of medicine.

5 **Use of the condom** Some measure of protection is afforded by use of the condom (sheath) as a contraceptive. This physical barrier around the penis reduces the likelihood of a pathogen passing to or from the female. This has implications when it comes to giving contraceptive advice. Since its introduction, the Pill has often been the first choice of contraceptive, particularly for young girls or women who are likely to be promiscuous. The rising incidence of STDs however is resulting in more widespread encouragement to use condoms, even as additional protection.

3.3 Syphilis

Causative agent and background to the disease

Syphilis is uncommon in Britain compared with many countries. It is most common in certain South American and African countries where infection rates are up to several hundred times higher than in Britain. The history of reported cases in Britain from 1925 to 1987 is shown in fig. 3.1. At the beginning of the century about 60 000 people per year died from syphilis in Britain, including 2000 infants. Today all expectant mothers are tested for syphilis, although it is rare.

Syphilis is caused by the bacterium *Treponema pallidum*. It belongs to an unusual group of bacteria called spirochaetes which have a long, slender spiral shape and move by flexing their bodies. The organism dies quickly in dry conditions and so far has proved impossible to culture in the laboratory.

Development and control of the disease

There are two forms of syphilis, namely **acquired** and **congenital syphilis**. The latter is transmitted from an infected mother across the placenta to the foetus while it is still in the uterus. Acquired syphilis is acquired by sexual contact. It develops over many years in recognised stages. These stages, together with signs and symptoms, treatment and prevention, are summarised in table 3.1.

The bacterium may enter the body through a cut or minor damage, such as may occur during sexual intercourse, to epithelia lining the urethra, vagina, rectum or mouth. The incubation period is usually 2 to 4 weeks, after which a sore (usually only one) called a **chancre** appears at the site of the original infection. A sample from the chancre shows spirochaetes and diagnosis can be confirmed immediately under a microscope. Treatment should ideally be given in this **primary stage**. The ease of diagnosis of the disease, together with its seriousness (which encourages patients to visit treatment clinics) helps to explain its relatively low incidence compared with gonorrhoea.

Table 3.1 Syphilis – stages in development, signs and symptoms, treatment and prevention.

	'Early stage' (infectious stage)		Latent stage	Tertiary syphilis	Cardiovascular syphilis	Neurosyphilis
	Primary syphilis	Secondary syphilis				
Time from original infection	2 to 4 weeks	8 to 12 weeks	2 years	3 to 10 years	10 to 20 years	30+ years
Duration	up to 4 weeks	2 years	approx. 1 to 10 years	approx. 10 years	until death	until death
Typical signs and symptoms	1 chancre (a highly infectious sore) at site of infection, painless	non-itchy pink rash on trunk, face, limbs (palms and soles) lasting several weeks. Swollen lymph nodes. Lesions in warm, moist areas, e.g. groin.	no signs or symptoms	many parts of body affected. Gummas (large lesions/ulcers) in skin, mouth, nose, throat. Bones and joints painful and crippled.	occurs in approx. 10% of untreated patients. Degeneration of base of aorta, coronary thrombosis, other complications.	insanity, blindness
Treatment	daily penicillin injections for up to 2 weeks. Cure rate over 95%. Follow-up visits for clinical examination and blood tests up to 2 years. Avoid sexual intercourse until tests negative.				penicillin and specialist treatment	
Prevention	see section 3.2 Gonorrhoea – the same principles apply.					

3.4   Non-specific urethritis and chlamydial infections

Introduction and causative agents

Non-specific urethritis, or NSU, is the commonest sexually transmitted disease in Britain. Recent statistics indicate that about 1 person in 500 catches NSU every year. The rise in reported cases in males during the period 1951 to 1985 is shown in fig. 3.4. Despite its high incidence, there is still a good deal to learn about the disease, particularly its incidence among women and its potential importance in women.

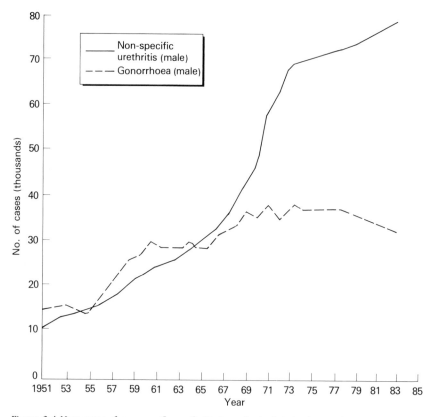

Figure 3.4 New cases of non-specific urethritis in males in Britain during the period of 1951 to 1985 based partly on *Lecture notes on sexually transmitted diseases*, R. Nicol Thin, Blackwell Scientific Publications Ltd. (1982)

The term non-specific urethritis has caused some confusion. **Urethritis** is an inflammation of the urethra which causes discomfort on urinating and which may be caused by a variety of infectious agents. In particular it is caused by gonococcus and is therefore a symptom of gonorrhoea. When the gonococcus bacterium has been shown *not* to be the cause, the condition is known as **non-specific urethritis** (NSU), (formerly **non-gonococcal urethritis**). It is now accepted that in about 50% of cases of NSU, the **causative agent** is a small bacterium called *Chlamydia trachomatis*. A different strain of the same bacterium causes trachoma, one of the commonest causes of blindness in the tropics. An estimated 5% of cases of NSU are caused by the bacterium *Ureaplasma* and the cause of the remaining 45% of cases is a mystery.

Further confusion arises from the fact that, although *Chlamydia* may infect women, it rarely causes urethritis and usually causes no signs or symptoms at all. NSU is therefore a disease that almost exclusively affects men. The term '**chlamydial infections**' is thus, perhaps, a better one to use than NSU. Another term used is non-specific genital infection (NSGI) which can be applied to men or women. The reported incidence in women is shown in fig. 3.3.

Signs, symptoms and effects

The incubation period is usually 2 to 3 weeks. In men the symptom is a mild burning or tingling sensation on passing urine and a sign is a slight discharge similar to that of gonorrhoea but less severe. These gradually disappear but the bacteria may still be active and the patient capable of passing it on.

In women the cervix is the usual site of early infection but there are normally no signs or symptoms. A slight increase in vaginal discharge may occur, and there may be mild discomfort when urinating. An uncommon long-term complication is development of pelvic inflammatory disease (PID) in which infection spreads to the Fallopian tubes, sometimes causing infertility. A woman suffering from PID may experience a lot of pain and constantly feel ill and run-down. It is most common in very young women, particularly after a pregnancy. PID can be caused by a variety of factors and is often linked with IUD insertions, pregnancy and abortion. It is difficult to know how common it is, as it is poorly diagnosed so far. The importance of *Chlamydia* as a cause is also difficult to establish because the *Chlamydia* test is not widespread (see Prevention). A further complication of chlamydial infections is that a mother may infect her baby during birth, resulting in an eye infection of the baby.

Control – treatment and prevention

Treatment Treatment is possible but the disease is difficult to identify, especially in women. A breakthrough in diagnosis occurred in late 1984. Rapid diagnosis (within minutes) became possible using monoclonal antibodies to *Chlamydia* antigens (see section 5.11). The antibodies are stained with a fluorescent marker (a technique known as immunofluorescence). They attach themselves to the *Chlamydia* bacteria and show up under the microscope due to their fluorescence. A sample taken from a patient can thus easily be tested in the laboratory. The new test cost about £2 on introduction. Large-scale testing of women would therefore be expensive although it is estimated that about 2000 cases of infertility a year could be prevented with a proper screening programme.

Once identified, treatment of the disease with an antibiotic is effective. Sexual intercourse should be avoided until a cure is effected.

Prevention Sexual contacts of identified cases should also be examined and treated if necessary. Principles of prevention in cases of STDs are discussed in section 3.2 Prevention.

3.5 Genital herpes (*Herpes genitalis*)

Causative agent and background information
Genital herpes is caused by a virus, the *Herpes simplex* virus. One strain (Type 1) causes cold sores on the lips and another strain (Type 2) causes genital infections. Numbers of infected people may have just started declining in England and Wales. In 1979, 9048 cases were reported in England and Wales, in 1985, 19 283 cases and in 1986, 19 210 cases.

Signs and symptoms
The characteristic sign is small red painful ulcers on the genitals of either sex. In the case of homosexuals the anus is affected. Fever, malaise and swelling of glands may also occur. Signs and symptoms disappear after a couple of weeks but return at irregular intervals in about half the patients, sometimes over many years and often at times when the patient is feeling run-down.

Control – treatment and prevention
There is no cure, although the ulcers can be treated to make them less painful. During attacks, sexual intercourse should be avoided to prevent transmission to the partner.

3.6 Genital warts
Warts may appear on the penis or vulva and are caused by a virus in the same way as warts on other parts of the body. They are mildly contagious and may therefore be spread by sexual intercourse. Warts can be removed by several applications of a special anti-wart paint available from doctors or by surgical removal. Doctors should be consulted for confirmation of diagnosis. There is some evidence that one particular wart virus, Papilloma 16 virus, is associated with, and hence may be a causative agent of, cervical cancer. Genital warts are a rapidly increasing disease (compare 25 104 new cases in England and Wales in 1979 with 53 638 in 1985, 69 126 in 1986 and over 75 000 in 1987.

3.7 Trichomonal infections (trichomoniasis)
Trichomonal infections are common and caused by a protozoan called *Trichomonas vaginalis*.

In women it causes a heavy, thin, yellow, unpleasant-smelling discharge from the vagina and there may be irritation or pain. It may occur without signs or symptoms. In men, signs and symptoms are usually absent.

Drug treatment is available. Both sexual partners should be treated. Follow-up visits to clinics and tracing of contacts are recommended.

3.8 Candidiasis or candidosis (vaginal thrush)

Causative agent
Candidiasis, or **thrush**, is caused by yeasts, mostly the yeast *Candida albicans*. Yeasts are unicellular fungi. The condition is very common (see fig. 3.2) and is not serious. Yeasts are normal inhabitants of various parts of the body, such as the mouth, gut and vagina. The environment of the vagina is usually acid due

to the activities of bacteria. This checks the growth of the yeast, but if the bacteria are destroyed the yeasts may multiply and become a problem. Widespread use of broad spectrum antibiotics is probably responsible for much of the rise in cases, although a decrease occurred in 1987.

Signs and symptoms

An increased vaginal discharge is observed which is usually white, thick and curdy. There may be intense itching, soreness and pain on passing urine. Men rarely show signs or symptoms, but may suffer mild irritation of the foreskin and tip of the penis. Mild urethritis is rare. The disease is not always sexually transmitted.

A woman is more susceptible if she is pregnant, diabetic, anaemic, using oral contraception, has recently had antibiotic treatment or certain other drugs such as corticosteroids, or has lowered resistance to disease through other factors. The increase in the disease until recently is probably due to increased use of broad spectrum antibiotics and possibly oral contraceptives.

Control – treatment and prevention

Treatment Antifungal tablets or cream may be inserted into the vagina. Tablets may also be taken by mouth.

Prevention Hygiene of the vulva is important. Thorough drying after washing, and wearing of cotton rather than synthetic underwear, helps prevent the damp conditions in which the fungus thrives. Patients should avoid sexual intercourse until cured. Vaginal deodorants should be avoided (they kill vaginal bacteria). The male partner may be the source of infection in which case he should be treated with antifungal cream. A switch from oral contraception may be recommended.

3.9 AIDS Acquired immune deficiency syndrome (HIV, Human immunodeficiency virus)

This disease will be dealt with under the heading of sexually transmitted diseases although, as will be made clear, sexual transmission is not the only method of transmission. Since its first appearance among homosexual men in New York and California in 1981, no disease has captured so much public attention as AIDS, the acquired immune deficiency syndrome. This concern arose because it is a disease affecting relatively young people which is, at present, invariably fatal. It probably originated in Central Africa but how is unclear. There are suggestions, for example, that it may have been transmitted to humans in a chance incident from other animals. The green monkey is known to harbour an almost identical virus, and sheep, horses and goats harbour similar viruses. The initial association of the disease with homosexuals and drug addicts added a social stigma to it which is extremely unfortunate because the inevitable moralising meant a slower response to the dangers that threaten the whole of society. The social stigma still exists. In December 1986, for example, the Chief Constable of Greater Manchester blamed the spread of AIDS on 'degenerate conduct' and said people at risk were 'swirling around in a cesspit of their own making'. A similar stigma attached to Africa as the possible origin, making the problem there more complex.

Causative agent

The AIDS virus (fig. 3.5) was identified in 1983 as an RNA virus of the type known as retroviruses. One subfamily of the retroviruses, the oncornaviruses (*onco*, cancer; *rna*, RNA) is known to cause leukaemia in humans, but the subfamily to which the AIDS virus belongs, the lentiviruses ('slow viruses'), had been little studied, having only been known to cause incurable lethal diseases in sheep, horses and goats. In 1986, the virus was named **HIV (human immunodeficiency virus)**, and a second, less virulent, form of the virus, HIV-2, was identified in Western Africa. This has now spread to Europe. HIV affects the immune system, replicating in a particular type of lymphocyte called the T4 cell. The role of lymphocytes and T-cells is discussed in section 5.5. T4 cells, or 'helper cells', 'help' or induce other T-cells, called killers, to fight invaders. Without them the body's immune system breaks down, leaving the patient exposed to a variety of diseases (see Signs, symptoms and nature of the disease). It is important to realise that infection with HIV does not necessarily result in AIDS. Some infected people remain symptomless and are termed carriers. They make antibodies against the virus which can be detected by a blood test. The

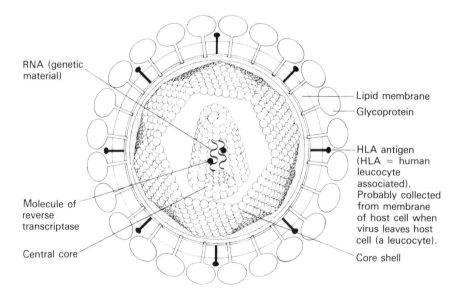

RNA (genetic material)

Lipid membrane

Glycoprotein

HLA antigen (HLA = human leucocyte associated). Probably collected from membrane of host cell when virus leaves host cell (a leucocyte).

Molecule of reverse transcriptase

Central core

Core shell

Figure 3.5 Diagram of the AIDS virus. At the centre of the virus is a **core** consisting of a hollow cone-shaped central core surrounded by a core shell. The central core is made of ribonucleoprotein (RNA + protein). Inside the cone is found RNA (the genetic material of the virus) and the enzyme reverse transcriptase, which makes DNA copies of the RNA. The core shell is made of protein. Around the core shell is a lipid membrane envelope containing glycoproteins (proteins combined with sugar). Proteins in the core or glycoproteins in the envelope may prove suitable for incorporation into vaccines. (This diagram by Gardiner first appeared in *New Scientist*, London, the weekly review of science and technology)

proportion of infected people who will go on to develop 'full-blown' AIDS is not known; the average incubation period for the virus is unknown, current estimates being eight to nine years.

Transmission and incidence

In the United Kingdom, HIV is mostly transmitted sexually by blood or semen. AIDS was originally associated with homosexual communities, notably in American cities like San Francisco, Los Angeles and Miami where there were high levels of promiscuity among homosexuals.

As noted above, HIV attacks blood cells (lymphocytes) and the disease is transmitted in infected blood. Transmission of retroviruses in general is not easy, and can occur only in special circumstances. The most common situations where contact is intimate enough are during anal intercourse (usually between homosexuals), and to a lesser extent during vaginal intercourse. HIV can also be transmitted by blood transfusions using blood from infected donors, use of non-sterile medical needles, and close contact with cuts and open wounds between infected and non-infected persons. It is present in semen, but seems to be transmitted less easily in semen than in blood, although four women in Australia had developed antibodies to HIV by 1986 after artificial insemination from an infected but symptomless male. The cervical secretions of infected women contain the virus and may therefore pass the disease to men. In some carriers, minute quantities of the virus can be detected in saliva, but experts agree that concentrations are so low that there is no risk of droplet infection or from kissing or giving the 'kiss of life'. No hospital workers involved with cases of AIDS have caught the disease from their patients. The virus cannot survive outside the body (unlike the flu virus, for example) and is destroyed by the acid in the stomach. There is no risk from cutlery, communion chalises, toilet seats, etc.

Anal intercourse can easily damage the delicate lining of the rectum, causing bleeding and infection by contaminated sperm or blood. Short-term physical transfer of cells from one anus to another may also occur on the penis of a promiscuous homosexual. Lesions are much rarer during vaginal intercourse because the walls of the vagina are tougher and do not bleed easily. However, the uterus contains delicate blood vessels and infected semen could easily reach these. An alarmingly large number of women are becoming infected in Central Africa, where almost equal numbers of men and women have the disease. In Africa, most rapid spread of the disease seems to be among the most sexually active members of the community, such as prostitutes, and this pattern may be occurring in the Western World. An estimated 2 to 20 million people carry HIV in Central, East and West Africa, a disease of pandemic proportions (precise figures are impossible to get). There may be variations in resistance to the disease between races due to genetic differences. In America over 17 000 cases of full-blown AIDS had been recorded up to 1986, with possibly more than 1 million as yet symptomless carriers.

Some figures for the U.K. are given in tables 3.2 and 3.3. In Europe, the countries France, W. Germany and the U.K. are the most affected.

After homosexuals, the second highest risk category is the intravenous drug

Table 3.2 AIDS cases in the U.K. and associated deaths.

Year	New cases	Running total of cases	New deaths	Running total of deaths
1982	3	3	3	3
1983	26	29	26	29
1984	77	106	60	89
1985	165	271	87	176
1986	339	610	117	293
1987				
1988				
1989				
1990				
1991				
1992				

Table 3.3 Total known U.K. cases of AIDS and HIV infection, by transmission characteristic, up to July 1988 (AIDS) or March 1988 (HIV infection).

Transmission characteristic	Cases of AIDS		*Known* cases of HIV infection*	
	No.	%	No.	%
Homosexual/bisexual	1279	83%	3901	46%
Injecting drug user	52	3%	1402	17%
Heterosexual	53	4%	394	5%
Haemophiliac/infected blood	128	8%	1184	14%
Other/several categories	29	2%	1562	18%
Total:	1541	100%	8443	100%

*Estimated number 40 000 to 200 000.

abuser. There are a quarter of a million heroin addicts in New York alone, of whom it is officially estimated about 60% have already been infected by the virus. In early 1986 research indicated that HIV had spread through Edinburgh's drug addicts at double the rate of New York, a fact largely attributable to the common practice of sharing needles and syringes in groups. Needles were in short supply in Edinburgh after pharmacists stopped their sale in 1982 in a bid to curb the use of drugs. An interesting moral and political dilemma then arose. Should sterile needles be made more readily available in order to reduce the risk of contracting HIV? Official government advertising, issued by the DHSS in March 1986, was deliberately low key, but implicitly admitted the problem: 'Injecting drug users are at risk if they share needles or other equipment. By far the best solution is not to inject at all. Those who persist, should not share equipment.' By 1987, more than half the intravenous drug users in the Edinburgh area had the virus (about 1000 people). The cost to the National Health Service of caring for the victims could be about £10 million.

A further factor to consider is the consensus among the world's experts that the disease will inevitably spread from drug addicts to the general population through sexual contact. Female addicts often turn to prostitution for a source of income and may pass on the virus in their cervical secretions. This is therefore potentially one of the most important routes of transmission to the general population. In Amsterdam, 100 000 needles and syringes were issued free in 1985 and the number of addicts has not increased. The medical authorities also provide free condoms to addicted prostitutes. There is evidence that these measures are restricting the spread of the virus among drug abusers. Encouraged by the DHSS, many areas of the U.K. now have free needle exchange schemes for those who inject drugs.

Early in the history of the disease, particularly in America, a common source of infection was blood transfusion from an infected donor. Now throughout the Western World all donated blood is screened for HIV infection. Haemophilia victims, who regularly require Factor VIII (the clotting agent) from blood, were particularly at risk. Factor VIII is now heat-treated to kill the virus (see Prevention).

Also at risk are the unborn babies of pregnant mothers who carry the virus. Unfortunately the babies have a very high rate of infection and subsequent development of AIDS, and risks to women are also increased by pregnancy. More than 20 babies had been born with the virus in Edinburgh by mid-1986, and abortion may be recommended if a pregnant woman is found to be carrying the virus.

Signs, symptoms and nature of the disease
The incubation period is normally 6 weeks to 6 months but may extend for years. The upper limit is not yet known. After this period, the person will show as HIV positive if a blood test is carried out. On entering the host cell, the viral RNA makes a DNA copy which is inserted into the host DNA. Here it can remain dormant, possibly for many years, before becoming activated to produce more viruses. Initially T4 helper cells are attacked, (see Causative agent above). For every 100 people infected, about a dozen per year show signs and symptoms and two fall ill from full-blown AIDS. At least 1 in 10 develop AIDS within 7 to 8 years.

First signs and symptoms are a short flu-like illness, followed by no signs or symptoms for months or years. AIDS involves a defect in the cell-mediated immune response (see section 5.5), hence the term 'immune deficiency'. Opportunistic infections then ensue: microorganisms that we normally live with and which we can normally easily destroy, may cause killer diseases. The cause of death is commonly a rare type of pneumonia caused by the agent *Pneumocystis carinii*. Many suffer a rare and disfiguring form of skin cancer known as Kaposi's sarcoma. Other common signs and symptoms of AIDS include weight loss, swollen lymph glands, fever, diarrhoea, dementia (brain deterioration), and certain forms of cancer. Severity of immune deficiency varies and bouts of illness may persist for years.

As well as affecting lymphocytes, HIV may directly infect brain cells causing irreversible dementia and eventual death. The brain shrinks, with a loss of memory and mental agility, and behavioural changes occur. Such cases may not be identified as being due to HIV because symptoms of immune deficiency and other illness may not occur. Long-term brain damage may emerge in the future as a common feature of the disease. It was estimated in 1988 that a high proportion, perhaps 50% of those infected with the virus, may eventually show long term brain disease, dementia or schizophrenia, even if these patients do not develop AIDS.

Control – treatment and prevention

An enormous international effort is being made to devise methods of treating and preventing the disease. There are two lines of research, one into developing drugs which can be used to cure or alleviate the disease, and one into developing a vaccine. Both approaches are at an early stage, and both require heavy financial investments. At the moment, modification of sexual behaviour is the only answer to the problem.

Treatment In the short term the aim is to develop drugs to inactivate the virus. A common principle in trying to control any pathogen with drugs is to try to block a vital part of the pathogen's metabolism which is not shared by the human host, thus killing the pathogen and leaving the victim unharmed. An obvious target in HIV is an enzyme called reverse transcriptase which is essential for replication of the virus. The enzyme converts the RNA of the virus into a DNA copy (reverse of normal transcription) once the RNA has infected a host cell. The enzyme is a characteristic feature only of certain viruses, including HIV, and is not present in normal human cells. The best-known drug in use by 1987 was zidovudine (formerly known as AZT), which slows progression of the disease and can attack the virus even in the brain (a major reservoir of infection).

The only other treatment possible at the moment is relief of symptoms where possible, and attempts to restrict the complications.

Prevention There are formidable obstacles to developing a vaccine because the virus constantly changes the detailed structure of its glycoprotein envelope, the main antigen of the virus. Many strains of the virus therefore exist in different parts of the world. The world's first full-scale trials of an HIV vaccine were authorised in the U.S.A. in August 1987. The vaccine contains virus coat proteins and trials are expected to take about 3 years. It is a genetically engineered vaccine whereby the gene coding for an antigenic protein from the virus coat was inserted into a virus which infects moths and butterflies. Infected caterpillars produce relatively large quantities of the desired protein (compare attempts to produce a malaria vaccine). This is a rapidly developing field and the interested reader is advised to keep up to date with progress by reading science journals such as *New Scientist* (AIDS Monitor section).

In the meantime there are some obvious precautions which can be followed in trying to prevent the disease. Abstention from anal intercourse is recommended for homosexuals, unless both partners have been tested for the virus and shown to be free from the AIDS antibodies characteristic of those infected. If anal intercourse is practised, use of a condom is a sensible precaution because it provides a mechanical barrier to transmission. There has been a noticeable drop in promiscuity among homosexuals in America and more recently in other western countries which will reduce the rate of transmission. Similarly, less promiscuity and, if sexual intercourse does occur, use of a condom, is recommended for heterosexuals.

The risk to drug abusers from non-sterile needles and syringes has been described. Apart from the control of drug abuse, which is considered in more detail in another book in this series (*Drugs, Alcohol and Mental Health* by Alan and Vicky Cornwell), a reduction in the spread of HIV could be brought about by the use of clean needles and syringes, a problem discussed above (Transmission and incidence).

Since October 1985 all blood donated in Britain has been tested for the presence of antibodies to HIV which indicates whether or not the donor is infected. Blood containing these antibodies is not used. There are 4800 haemophiliacs in Britain who rely on a regular supply of Factor VIII protein, the clotting agent, from blood. A heat treatment of the blood plasma containing Factor VIII of 68°C for 24 hours has been shown to kill HIV without denaturing the Factor VIII protein. This has been routine procedure since February 1985. More than 1000 haemophiliacs were given HIV before the procedure was introduced.

Education about the disease is an important factor in its prevention. Here the media have an important role to play, particularly in reassuring the public about the real risks. The early social ostracising of those shown to have been infected, including some unfortunate haemophiliacs, was no doubt due in part to the sensational treatment of the subject in the press. There is no evidence that infection can occur by droplet infection through the nose or mouth, or by casual contact. Healthcare staff who tend AIDS patients have never contracted the disease in this way. The British government was slow to launch a full-scale education programme partly for financial reasons but partly perhaps because of the social stigma attached to the disease. Spending money to promote advice on sex may offend some people and the need for sexually explicit advertising is mistakenly regarded in some quarters as obscene. The phrase 'anal intercourse' was replaced by 'rectal sex' in the official advertisement launched in 1986 by the DHSS. This was part of an official public health campaign costing £2 million. At the same time Sweden, with a population of 8 million, had invested £20 million in advertising. A Cabinet committee set up to deal with AIDS in Britain had, however, allocated funds of this order by the end of 1986. Twenty-three million householders received AIDS leaflets in 1987 and surveys indicated that about 70% of people read them. Gradually social taboos are breaking down. For example, 70% of the British public are now reported to be in favour of advertising condoms on TV. By 1988 there was evidence that new infections among homosexuals were declining in the U.K. However, among the population as a whole, there had been no significant increase in the number of condoms being used.

Social implications of the disease

AIDS, more than most diseases, requires a profound social as well as medical response. Apart from the challenge of control, which has been discussed, there is the challenge of care for people with AIDS. The average cost to the NHS is currently about £20 000 per patient from diagnosis to death, and there are also costs to Social Services in providing home helps, counselling, residential and day-care provisions and training of staff. Caring for people with AIDS is also extremely exhausting for medical staff given the resources available.

It is estimated that in the U.S.A., HIV will be costing $2000 million a year by 1990 and that 20% of public hospital beds will be filled with AIDS patients. (The estimate for Britain is £30 million per year.) Clearly the financial cost alone will be enormous for society. Funds on this scale are simply not available in developing countries.

What services should be set up to help people, including those that have been identified as HIV-antibody positive? Fear, loneliness and subsequent isolation can easily strike in the absence of support in some cases. In some areas counselling groups have been set up, for example, by the Lighthouse Hospice in S.W. London. Their new building, completed in 1988, includes a training centre, restaurant, counselling rooms and 26 hospice beds for patients. If people with AIDS wish to remain in their own homes, as most do, for as long as possible, many volunteers are needed in the community to provide company, and emotional and practical support. Above all, understanding is required.

Another factor to consider is the fact that people with AIDS are often in their middle years, when they are normally making their most significant contributions to society. Thus there is a tragic waste for society as well as individuals. Dr Tony Pinching of St Mary's Hospital in Paddington, London, quotes a case from Africa of grandparents caring for 11 grandchildren because 8 members of the parent generation have died of AIDS.

Some moral questions which have been raised, and which could be discussed are:

1. Should it be legal to sample and test blood for HIV antibodies without a patient's knowledge or consent?
2. Should there be compensation for those who have been infected by blood transfusions, notably haemophiliacs?
3. Should building societies and life insurance companies discriminate against homosexuals, or those who have had HIV tests, even if the latter have proved *negative*?
4. Should the Church encourage homosexual marriages (with consequent encouragement of long-term sexual partners)?
5. What is the role of the Church?

The challenge now is to think very carefully about our own attitudes as individuals, to identify and respond to local needs and to consider the implications of the fact that AIDS and the suffering it causes transcends international boundaries. For further information see the references at the end of this book.

3.10   Hepatitis A and B

Hepatitis A and B are liver infections caused by viruses. They are not strictly speaking sexually transmitted diseases although they can be transmitted as a result of sexual intercourse.

Hepatitis A is rare in Britain. It is commonly faecal-borne and is not normally a serious disease, causing flu-like symptoms and jaundice. Hepatitis B, however, has serious risks associated with it, and may cause death. It may be spread in similar ways to hepatitis A and may cause similar signs and symptoms. One of the particular problems of the disease is that many people remain carriers. It is commonly spread by contact with infected blood and, like AIDS, is therefore particularly associated with drug abusers. No one who is known to have had the disease is permitted to donate blood. The virus is contained in body secretions like saliva, semen and vaginal discharges. Sexual transmission among male homosexuals is now the main method of spread in the western world. A vaccine is available but it is expensive (£75 in 1986) and prescriptions for homosexuals are often refused if the risks are not regarded as high enough. 80% of homosexuals in London have been exposed to hepatitis B.

4 Malaria

4.1 Introduction

Throughout recorded history, malaria has been one of the world's worst killer diseases, and it remains so even today. In the 1950s the annual death toll world-wide was estimated at 2.5 million, with 250 million cases annually. In 1956, the World Health Organisation launched a campaign to rid the world finally of malaria, and since the eradication of smallpox in 1978 has given this even greater priority. However its elimination has proved a far more intractable problem than eradicating smallpox. Indeed, after early successes during the 1960s there has been a resurgence of the disease and there were more cases in 1980 than in 1965. For example, 5.8 million cases were reported in India in 1976 compared with 40 000 in 1966. It still exists in about 100 countries, mainly in Africa, Central and South America, and Asia. In Africa 1 million people a year (10% of those infected), mainly infants and children, die from the disease. About 200 to 400 million people a year are currently affected. The economic poverty of the most seriously affected countries compounds the problem of developing effective control measures (see section 4.6). A study of malaria provides not only a fascinating picture of a battle by biologists against a disease, but illustrates vividly how important social, economic and political influences can be in controlling disease.

4.2 Causative agent

Malaria is caused by the protozoan parasite *Plasmodium*. Protozoa are unicellular organisms (see table 1.6). Two species of *Plasmodium* are commonly involved, *Plasmodium vivax* and *Plasmodium falciparum*, the latter of which is the more prevalent and more lethal.

   P. vivax (benign tertian malaria) is found in the subtropics, whereas *P. falciparum* (malignant tertian malaria) occurs in both the tropics and subtropics, and is the largest single cause of death in Africa. Two other *Plasmodium* species are known to cause malaria in humans, but are uncommon.

4.3 Transmission

Malaria is transmitted (*not* caused) by female mosquitoes of the genus *Anopheles*. The mosquito is described as a **vector**, that is an organism that transmits disease from one person to another or from an infected animal to a human.

4.4 Life cycle of *Plasmodium*

The life cycle of *Plasmodium*, illustrated in fig. 4.1, is complex and involves a series of multiplication stages in both its human host and its vector, the mosquito. These stages compensate for the large losses of numbers that inevitably occur in a life cycle that involves transfer from one host species to another.

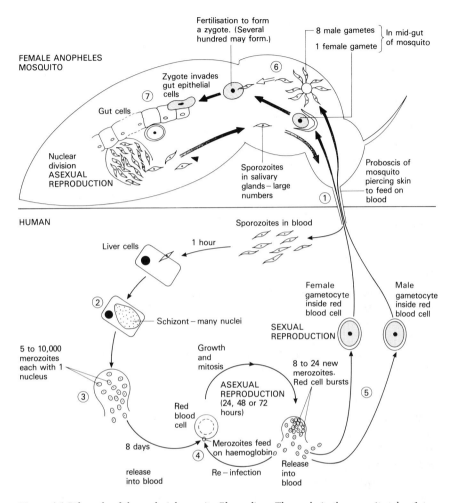

Figure 4.1 Life cycle of the malarial parasite *Plasmodium*. The cycle *in the mosquito* takes 1 to 2 weeks on average

Circadian rhythms

The asexual cycle in the red blood cells is synchronised so that merozoites are released at 24, 48 or 72 hour intervals, depending on the species of malaria parasite. Release coincides with the fever characteristic of malaria; the cycle may take place many times. Release is linked with the 24 hour cycle of body temperature and usually takes place during late afternoon. Twenty-four hour cycles are called circadian rhythms. Merozoites develop into gametocytes by the early evening of the following day (the process takes slightly longer than 24 hours). This is the time when mosquitoes normally feed and since release of merozoites induces fever, the hot body of the victim will effectively attract mosquitoes. Maximum efficiency of transfer from the human host to the vector is thus achieved.

4.5   Signs and symptoms of malignant tertian malaria (*P. falciparum*)

The incubation period of *P. falciparum* is 8 to 14 days. The first signs and symptoms occur when the parasite leaves the liver cells and enters the blood, and are similar to flu, namely headache, fever and general body pain, accompanied sometimes by vomiting. The asexual cycle in red blood cells is 48 hours. Fevers may therefore occur regularly at 48 hour intervals, but may also be more frequent and irregular. For about 2 hours after release of the merozoites, the patient feels cold and shivers violently. The temperature then rises steeply to about 40°C (104°F) and after about 4 hours the patient starts to sweat profusely for a further 2 to 4 hours while the temperature drops to normal.

Signs and symptoms are diverse and may imitate other illnesses. Some are due to damaged blood cells blocking blood vessels, which may rupture, causing internal bleeding. Organs or tissues thus cut off from blood are damaged by oxygen starvation. Kidneys, liver, lungs and brain are commonly affected. If blood vessels in the brain are blocked, cerebral malaria ensues; this is particularly common among children. The spleen and liver, where red cells are removed by phagocytes, are enlarged. If untreated, anything up to a dozen bouts of fever may be experienced. The anaemia, and acute exhaustion which results, is responsible for much of the high death rate. Subsequently, even minor illnesses may be fatal to the weakened individual, another reason why so many children die. As with other illnesses, those already suffering from malnutrition are at greater risk of dying.

P. falciparum does not remain dormant within the body, unlike some other species, and reinfection can only occur from fresh mosquito bites. Some resistance will have been gained to the original strain of the parasite, but many strains exist and complete resistance is never achieved.

4.6   Control of malaria

The attempts of the World Health Organisation to eradicate malaria have been mentioned in section 4.1. Strategies for control include the control of mosquitoes and development of antimalarial drugs, but long-term, total eradication depends on development of a successful vaccine. It will be seen how important it is for the life cycle of a parasite to be understood in as much detail as possible in order to achieve effective control.

Control of mosquitoes

Teams of specially trained staff are employed to attack the mosquito at several points in its life cycle. The mosquito lays its eggs in still water and has an aquatic larval stage. Areas of open water such as swamps, marshes, gutters, ditches, ponds, lakes, drains, tins and cisterns are sprayed with oil and an insecticide such as DDT. Oil forms a thin layer on the surface of the water which prevents the breathing tube of the mosquito larva from acquiring oxygen from the air. Drainage of swamps is sometimes carried out. These measures inevitably cause environmental damage, destroying habitats and, in the case of DDT, leading to harmful build up of insecticide in food chains. A difficult balance, therefore, has to be struck between environmental protection and disease control. Biological control is less harmful to the environment but less effective. For example, fish that feed on mosquito larvae have been introduced in some tropical lakes and a bacterium that infects and kills the larvae has also been used. Regular treatment of breeding grounds is one of the most effective ways of controlling malaria, but unfortunately one of the most expensive. Poor, rural areas may not therefore be tackled on economic grounds.

At the same time, attacks on the adult mosquito can be carried out. Mosquitoes rest during the day, typically in sheltered positions in or outside houses. Systematic spraying of resting places with an insecticide is very effective. Persistent insecticides, such as DDT, which remain active for long periods, will continue to kill mosquitoes for some time after spraying. DDT has the advantage of being cheap, easy to produce, and highly effective, but environmentally is one of the most damaging insecticides. More expensive, but safer, products such as the organophosphates (e.g. Malathion) and carbamates are now more commonly used for house spraying.

The resurgence of malaria mentioned in the introduction has been largely due to the emergence of insecticide-resistant mosquitoes.

Sleeping under mosquito nets and covering windows and doors with gauze are further sensible precautions against mosquitoes biting.

Anti-malarial drugs

Another strategy is to attack the parasite once it has infected the human host. The chemical quinine was used in the past, but is seldom used now because it has toxic side effects. Safer, synthetic drugs are used, most commonly chloroquine. These act against the stages in the red blood cells, and can cure attacks by *P. falciparum*. However, other species can remain dormant in the liver and must be attacked by other drugs.

Theoretically, malaria could be eradicated if all members of a population took these drugs regularly. In practice, however, this would be impossible to organise due mainly to lack of human resources and expense. Recently, strains of malaria have appeared which show multiple resistance to the drugs and the first new drugs for 30 years are having to be developed.

As malaria has been eliminated in the richer, developed countries, so there has been less incentive among drugs companies to develop new drugs because the poorer countries cannot afford to pay the high prices demanded. Economic prosperity is therefore an important component of control, as is political intervention in the form of financial aid. The role of the WHO is vital in this area.

Use of drugs to *prevent*, rather than cure, malaria is also possible. These can be taken, for example, before and during a visit to an area where malaria is endemic. *Paludrine* (whose active ingredient is proguanil) is the best known.

Vaccination

The aim with vaccination is to stimulate the body's own defence system into producing antibodies that will attack the antigens of the parasite, thus bringing about its death. Antibodies are produced by people with the disease but this does not seem to prevent them from suffering repeated attacks, albeit progressively milder ones, or from being reinfected by mosquitoes with other strains of the parasite. New methods in molecular biology offer renewed hopes of countering the parasite's own defences. Knowledge of the immune system (see chapter 5) is necessary to understand these new methods. The parasite is most vulnerable to antibodies when free and not contained within liver cells or red blood cells. This occurs at three stages, the sporozoite, merozoite and gamete stages. Each has its own characteristic antigens. Antisporozoite vaccine would break the link from mosquito to humans; antimerozoite vaccine would lead to an attack on the parasite in mid-infection; antigamete vaccine would be injected into humans, and the antibodies it induced would be taken up with gametocytes by the mosquito and kill the gametes when they emerged in the mosquito. This would break the link from humans to mosquito. All these approaches have been tried. For example, a vaccine containing sporozoites attenuated ('crippled') by exposure to radiation has had limited success. However, sporozoites cannot be produced on the scale required for commercial development. An alternative approach is to isolate that part of the sporozoite which is antigenic and *synthesise* large quantities of it for use as a vaccine. This involves the techniques of genetic engineering and a possible procedure is described in fig. 5.7. A similar approach may succeed for merozoites or gametes.

Unfortunately, many of the antigens so far discovered induce production of antibodies that do not kill the parasite. This explains why natural infection rarely produces protective immunity. The reasons for this are complex and varied. One problem is that the asexual stage can probably change its surface antigens over a period of time, requiring the host to make new antibodies. The parasite thus keeps 'one step ahead' of the host's immune system. It seems that the development of vaccines will continue to be a difficult problem.

5 Immunology

5.1 Introduction

Our environment contains a large number of potentially harmful microorganisms against which the body must defend itself. The human body provides in many respects an ideal location for the growth and replication of microorganisms. For example, the blood is kept at a constant temperature, pH, osmotic potential and ionic concentration and contains readily available nutrients. The first line of defence is the body surface. The skin is not only a physical barrier, but secretes its own defensive chemicals and has its own commensal organisms which offer a degree of protection. Other initial barriers to entry include the acid in the stomach; cilia and mucus in the respiratory pathway; and lysozyme (a hydrolytic enzyme) in tears, nasal secretions and saliva. This chapter, however, is concerned with the response of the body to foreign material which penetrates these barriers. Above all, it will be concerned with the white blood cells, whose role it is to eliminate this foreign material. Foreign material includes not only microorganisms but other material such as pollen, venom, grafted human tissue and transplanted organs. Functionally, 98% of white blood cells fall into two categories, phagocytes and lymphocytes. A further 2% of white blood cells are concerned with specialised activities such as allergic and inflammatory responses.

5.2 Phagocytes

Phagocytes are cells that carry out **phagocytosis**, which is the process by which cells engulf particles. Once inside the cell, the particles are digested, and thus destroyed, by lysosomal enzymes. Like all blood cells, phagocytes are derived from bone marrow cells called stem cells. Two main types can be recognised with a microscope (fig. 5.1), namely polymorphonuclear granulocytes and monocytes (which develop into macrophages).

Macrophages (see fig. 5.1) ('rubbish collectors') form a network of cells in many organs of the body. Collectively the network is called the reticulo-endothelial system (RES). It is concentrated in the endothelial layer of blood capillaries, in connective tissue, in the lung, liver, spleen and lymph nodes, kidney glomerulus, brain, synovial cavities and bone (osteoclasts). Overall they are strategically placed to intercept and remove foreign material, for example, invading micro-organisms or dust from the lungs.

Phagocytes represent the front line of defence among white blood cells. They act in the critical period between initial infection and the immune response by lymphocytes. Their numbers increase rapidly on infection. They accumulate at wounds and may be killed by toxins produced by bacteria. A collection of dead white blood cells and dead bacteria forms pus. Apart from the digestion of invading microorganisms, phagocytes clear up the dead cells remaining after an immune response and remove old or damaged parts of the body. They are also involved in lymphocyte activation, by processing and presenting antigens, and inflammatory and fever responses.

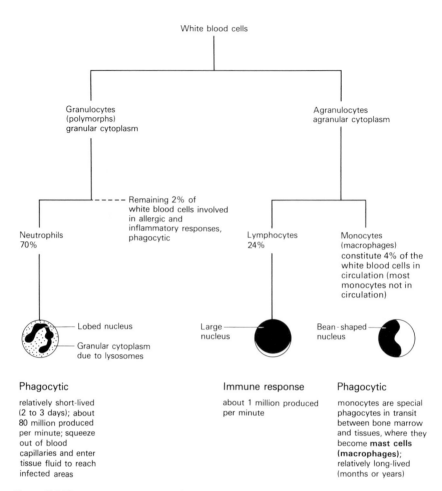

Figure 5.1 The most common types of white blood cells

5.3 The complement system

Phagocytes have to be able to recognise and be attracted to the particles they should engulf. Their ability to do this is greatly enhanced by the **complement system**. Complement is a group of about 20 soluble proteins found in the blood plasma, and it has a variety of functions, including control of inflammation. The system is activated by molecules in the surfaces of the invading microorganisms.

1 Some complement proteins coat the surfaces of bacteria, a process called **opsonisation**. Such proteins are called **opsonins** (some antibodies also act as opsonins). This allows phagocytes to recognise bacteria and stimulates phagocytosis.

2 Some complement proteins attract phagocytes to the site of infection

by a process of chemotaxis, the phagocyte moving down a concentration gradient of the chemical.

3 Another group of complement proteins destroys bacteria by making holes in their cell membranes causing them to swell and burst (**lysis**).

5.4 The immune response, antibodies and antigens

A second line of defence is provided by the immune response, which involves the white blood cells known as lymphocytes (see fig. 5.1). The **immune response** is the production of antibodies in response to antigens. An **antibody** is a glycoprotein of the type known as immunoglobulins which is synthesised in response to **antigens**. It has a specific recognition of the antigen, to which it binds, rather like a key in a lock. It is found in the blood plasma and tissue fluids. Five distinct classes of immunoglobulin molecule (Ig) occur in humans, namely IgG, IgA, IgM, IgD and IgE. Each has the same basic structure, illustrated in fig. 5.2. Each molecule is Y-shaped and made up of 4 polypeptide chains, 2 identical short (light) chains and 2 identical long (heavy) chains. The latter are shown shaded in fig 5.2. Each chain has a **variable** domain (region) at one end and a **constant** domain at the other. The variable region has a variable amino acid sequence and this variation gives the specificity needed to bind different antigens. The antibody binding site has a shape which specifically matches the shape of part of the antigen molecule. Several million different variants can be

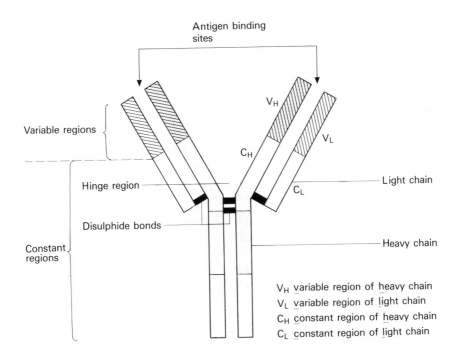

Figure 5.2 Basic structure of an antibody. In the variable regions the amino acid sequence is variable and unique for a given antibody. In the constant regions it is constant for each class of antibody

produced, so that any foreign antigen can be recognised, even if the body has never previously been exposed to it. The generation of this diversity is controlled by the genes that code for antibody proteins. The constant region is also important. It binds to host cells, particularly phagocytes, and may also activate or bind to complement protein. This is necessary because simple binding of the antibody to an antigen is usually not sufficient to destroy the microbe.

All antibodies have a carbohydrate portion attached to the protein, not shown in fig. 5.2 because its position is variable among the 5 classes. Antibodies are therefore glycoproteins.

An **antigen** is a molecule which causes the formation of an antibody. Antigens are usually proteins, polysaccharides or glycoproteins and are found either bound to the surfaces of cells (or viruses) or as free molecules. It is important to understand that *all* cells have these marker molecules in their surfaces and that they often have the important function of enabling cells to recognise other cells. The body has taken advantage of this fact because it has evolved a means of recognising its own antigens so these are not attacked, but of recognising and attacking *foreign* antigens, which *are* attacked.

5.5 Origins and roles of lymphocytes

Lymphocytes are part of the **lymphoid system**, which is made up of the lymphoid organs and lymphoid tissues (see fig. 5.3). These are linked by lymphatic vessels which, together with the lymphoid system make up the lymphatic system. Only the lymphoid system will be considered in this book. Two types of lymphocyte develop, the T-lymphocytes (T cells) and B-lymphocytes (B cells). Both types can be traced back to stem cells in the bone marrow, and both respond to antigens by multiplying and undergoing fundamental changes.

T cells and the cell-mediated response

T cells are so-called because they visit the thymus gland after production in the bone marrow. The thymus gland is located in the thorax (fig. 5.3) just above the heart. It starts to function in the foetus and is at its most active just after birth. During childhood it decreases in size and eventually ceases to function.

Once inside the thymus gland, the stem cells develop into thymocytes. These either remain inside the thymus gland or develop into T-lymphocytes, enter the circulation and migrate to the lymphoid tissues such as the lymph nodes and spleen. They also circulate in the blood and tissue fluids. During development in the thymus gland T cells are modified for their particular functions. This includes development of specific receptor sites on the cells which are essential in their recognition of other cells or molecules. For example, all mature T cells either have the T4 molecule (T4 cells) or the T8 molecule (T8 cells), giving them different functions.

When a T cell recognises an antigen, it divides to form a clone of identical cells all of which can bind to that antigen. Some are effector cells and some memory cells (see fig 5.5). Details of how the antigen-bearing cell or antigen molecule is destroyed are too complex for full consideration here, and are still the subject of research. Figure 5.4 illustrates some of this complexity. Basically,

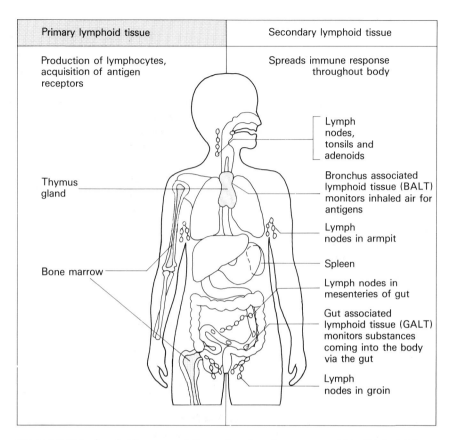

Primary lymphoid tissue	Secondary lymphoid tissue
Production of lymphocytes, acquisition of antigen receptors	Spreads immune response throughout body

Lymph nodes, tonsils and adenoids

Bronchus associated lymphoid tissue (BALT) monitors inhaled air for antigens

Thymus gland

Lymph nodes in armpit

Spleen

Bone marrow

Lymph nodes in mesenteries of gut

Gut associated lymphoid tissue (GALT) monitors substances coming into the body via the gut

Lymph nodes in groin

Figure 5.3 Major lymphoid organs and tissues; lymph nodes are more widely distributed than shown. They monitor tissue fluids returning as lymph to the circulation. Courtesy of Roitt, Brostoff and Male and Gower Medical Publishing

however, the response is described as cell-mediated immunity because it involves whole cells such as T-lymphocytes or macrophages, and not free antibodies. The receptor (recognition) sites in the membranes of the T-lymphocytes are equivalent to antibodies in that they are variable and specific for particular antigens. They appear to be incomplete antibody molecules, still possessing the important variable regions. Cell-mediated immunity interacts with humoral immunity which is discussed below.

B cells and the humoral response

B cells are derived from stem cells in the bone marrow. In birds they originate in lymphoid tissue in a branch of the gut called the bursa (hence B cells). The bursa as a structure does not exist in mammals but equivalent tissue does occur. Maturation of B cells takes place in lymphoid tissues, mainly in the liver, spleen or lymph nodes, and some B cells are found circulating in the blood and tissue fluids. Inside B cells, antibodies are produced which are inserted into the cell membrane where they act as specific antigen receptors. A cell is activated when antigen binds to it. As with T cells, the B cell then multiplies to produce

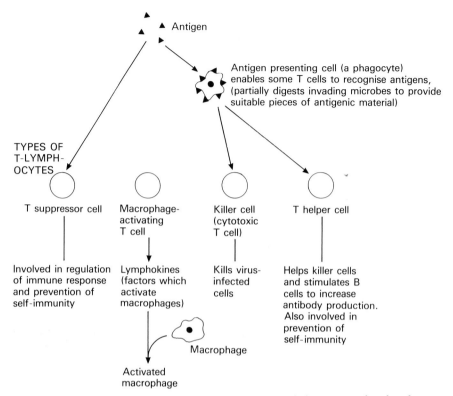

Figure 5.4 Cell-mediated immunity; it involves lymphocytes and phagocytes rather than free antibodies. T suppressor and T helper cells regulate the immune response – in effect the 'conductors of the orchestra'; HIV attacks T helper cells

many identical copies of itself (a clone). Some of these cells are effector cells called **plasma cells** and some are memory cells (see fig. 5.5). The plasma cells live for only a few days but during that time produce identical antibodies at a rapid rate (about 2000 molecules per second per cell). The plasma cells usually remain in the lymphoid tissue but their antibodies are released into the blood plasma and tissue fluids. This is described as a **humoral response** – the term 'humoral' is used to describe chemicals such as hormones and antibodies that circulate in *fluid*. Figure 5.5 summarises the main types of the cell-mediated and humoral responses.

Antibodies function in various ways, the relative importance of which varies from infection to infection. These are summarised below.

1 **Opsonisation**

Opsonisation (see section 5.3) involves coating bacteria with antibody molecules. The constant region of the antibody can then bind to phagocytes, which devour the bacteria.

2 **Neutralisation**

Antibodies may combine with microorganisms and neutralise their ability to attach to susceptible cells. In cases where bacteria produce toxins, such as with diphtheria, tetanus and scarlet fever, the antibody may neutralise the toxins.

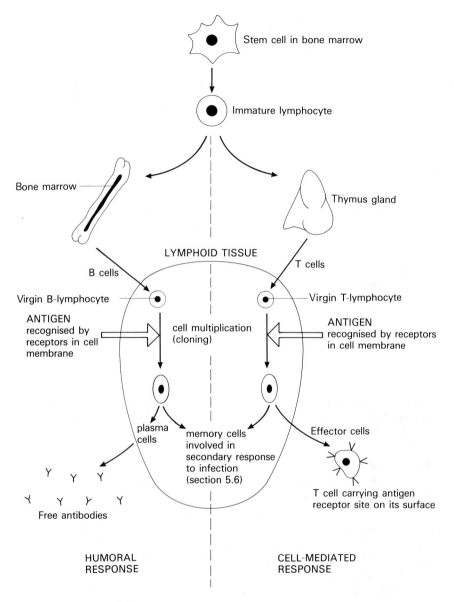

Figure 5.5 Summary of the main stages of the cell-mediated and humoral immune responses

3 **Interaction with complement and lysis**
Antibodies may combine with the microorganism and then bind complement. This leads to lysis (bursting) of the microorganism because its cell membrane is damaged.

4 **Agglutination**
Antibodies sometimes **agglutinate** microorganisms, that is cause them to stick together in clumps, linked by antibodies. This makes phagocytosis more efficient.

5.6 The immune system has a memory

After the first exposure to a given antigen the body takes some time to react and to produce antibodies as shown in fig. 5.6. This is the **primary response**. If the foreign material is a pathogen, the person may suffer the disease before the body can 'fight off' the attack. However, during this period memory cells are produced which persist after the antigen has disappeared. If the body later receives a second exposure to the antigen the memory cells are stimulated to clone themselves and the body's response is not only much more rapid but also larger. This is called the **secondary response**. Different classes of antibody are involved in these responses, as shown in fig. 5.6. Successive exposures to antigens generally bring about progressively greater responses. As will be seen, this 'immunological memory' is the principle upon which vaccination is based.

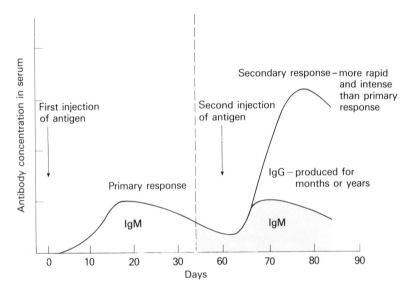

Figure 5.6 Primary and secondary responses to antigen, from Green, Stout and Taylor, *Biological Science* CUP (1985)

5.7 Types of immunity

Immunity may be classified as active or passive, and natural or artificial. A summary of types of immunity is given in table 5.1.

Active immunity

Active immunity occurs when the body produces *its own* antibodies in response to antigens. After the primary response the body has acquired immunity, and subsequent infections are usually repelled immediately (section 5.6). Protection usually lasts a long time, sometimes even for life.

This can be taken advantage of by supplying antigens artificially to build up the body's resistance to a disease. Since the antigen is only a small part of the infective agent, usually part of its surface, there are various methods, discussed

Table 5.1 Summary of different types of immunity.

	ACTIVE *antigens received*	*PASSIVE* *antibodies received*
NATURAL	NATURAL ACTIVE e.g. suffering a disease, rejecting a transplant	NATURAL PASSIVE from mother via placenta, colostrum or milk
ARTIFICIAL (IMMUNISATION)	ARTIFICIAL ACTIVE vaccination (injection of antigens)	ARTIFICIAL PASSIVE injection of antibodies

below, for preparing harmless antigen preparations. Such preparations are called **vaccines** and administering the vaccine is called **vaccination**. Vaccination can therefore be defined as a process that confers **artificial active immunity**. The process of providing artificial immunity is called **immunisation**. Immunisation also includes administering antibodies artificially (see Artificial passive immunity below).

Vaccines may be injected (inoculated) or taken orally. Often a second, 'booster', dose is needed to enhance the body's response and improve protection. Further booster doses may be recommended after some time (see for example polio vaccine, table 5.2).

In preparing vaccines, the aim is to make a preparation which contains suitable antigens of the organism against which protection is required, and yet which does not contain organisms capable of growing and multiplying normally and hence causing the disease.

Vaccines are traditionally made in one of 3 ways:

1 **Killed vaccines** A procedure is devised which will kill the organism concerned without altering the structure of the relevant antigens. Heat treatment (e.g. cholera vaccine) and exposure to certain chemicals such as phenol are commonly used. Examples described in chapter 2 include influenza A and B (section 2.1), and cholera (section 2.4). Whooping cough vaccine contains dead bacteria (section 5.9).

2 **Live vaccines** The modern trend is towards live vaccines. In most cases an **attenuated** organism is used, that is, one that has been 'crippled'. It is still living, but is no longer capable of growing and multiplying at the normal rate, and is destroyed by the body's defences before it can cause disease. As with killed vaccines this may be achieved by heat or chemical treatment. The advantage over killed vaccines is that live vaccines more closely mimic a natural infection. Because the organism multiplies inside the body, less has to be provided initially and the body often mounts a better, more longlasting response. Booster doses may not be necessary. In fact, the classical primary and secondary responses described in section 5.6 are usually indistinguishable, as with natural infections, because the antigen builds up and acts as a stimulus over a number of days.

Examples of live vaccines are described in chapter 2 for polio (section 2.2) and tuberculosis (section 2.5). Other diseases against which attenuated vaccines are used include the virus diseases measles, rubella (german measles), the common cold (not a very effective vaccine since there are so many strains of the virus), mumps, yellow fever and rabies. With smallpox an attenuated virus was *not* used, but a related, harmless virus (*Vaccinia*). Influenza is the only viral disease for which a killed vaccine is still used.

3 **Toxoids** A **toxoid** is an inactivated toxin. The bacteria responsible for tetanus and diphtheria have their lethal effects by producing powerful toxins (poisons), not by causing tissue damage at the site of infection. The toxins produce an immune response. When exposed to formalin, the toxin is rendered inactive, although will still induce production of antibodies when injected into the body. This inactive toxin is used in vaccines. From being a feared killer disease, particularly of young children, diphtheria has now almost been wiped out by the vaccination programme in Britain.

New developments in producing vaccines

Most of the vaccines described so far have been in use for many years, but after a comparative lull in vaccine development, new impetus has been gained by the important and exciting new techniques being developed in molecular biology and genetic engineering. There are frequent reports in *New Scientist* about development of new vaccines, particularly in the fight against AIDS and the common tropical diseases such as malaria (section 4.6), blood fluke (schistosomiasis) and leprosy. We are undoubtedly at the eve of a new era in disease control.

One approach is to produce large quantities of antigen by techniques of genetic engineering. The object is to transfer the gene coding for the antigen into a harmless bacterium such as *E. coli* and thus get commercial production of antigens on a large scale (see fig. 5.7). The first human trials of genetically engineered vaccine against cholera and typhoid began in Australia in 1986. The vaccine is taken orally and is expected to give lifelong immunity against cholera. It was hoped that it would be in general use by 1988. Estimated cost of development was $50 million!

If an antigen is simple enough, an alternative to genetic engineering is to synthesise it chemically, an approach now being adopted for an anti-hepatitis B vaccine (see section 3.10). All the approaches mentioned are being explored in the search for a vaccine against HIV.

Passive immunity

Passive immunity occurs when the body receives antibodies from some external source, either artificially or naturally. The body receives *immediate* protection, but it is *short-lived* because the body has not learned to make its own antibodies, and once the antibodies are broken down in the normal way, they cannot be replaced.

Natural passive immunity can only be obtained from the mother, either by

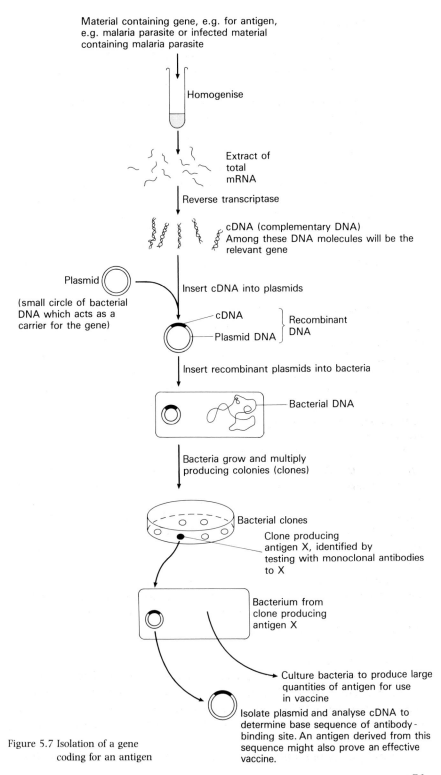

Figure 5.7 Isolation of a gene
coding for an antigen

the foetus when antibodies cross the placenta, or by the breast-fed infant through the mother's colostrum, an antibody-rich secretion produced instead of milk in the first day or two after birth. The foetus and the new-born baby therefore gain protection against the same diseases as the mother. This is important because the baby's own immune system takes several months to become effective after birth.

Artificial passive immunity is a form of immunisation (artificial immunity) in which antibodies are injected rather than antigens. Because of problems with allergic responses it is now used only against diphtheria and tetanus toxins and not directly against bacteria, having been replaced by antibiotics. It is possible to raise antibodies to the toxins by injecting small doses of the toxins into horses. Once the horse has developed antibodies, its blood serum, containing the antibodies, can be extracted and purified for use. The preparation is called an **antiserum**. Since tetanus can occur through contaminated wounds, particularly deep wounds, and particularly if soil has entered the wound, it is standard practice to give tetanus antibodies in these cases if the person has not been vaccinated.

Vaccination against tetanus and diphtheria is to be preferred and is part of the standard childhood programme of vaccinations (table 5.2). The use of monoclonal antibodies is resulting in a resurgence of interest in antibody treatment (see section 5.11).

5.8 The smallpox story

The classic example of how effective a vaccination programme can be is the campaign to eradicate smallpox, once a dreaded disease throughout the world and, since 1977, when the last case was reported in Somalia, deemed eradicated by the World Health Organisation. The eradication programme was started at the same time as that for malaria by the WHO in 1956.

The smallpox virus now survives only in a few carefully controlled laboratories for research purposes, and here the workers still receive vaccination. The final stages of eradication involved careful tracing and surveillance of all contacts of anyone reported to have the disease, and 'ring vaccination' whereby efforts were concentrated on vaccinating everyone who could possibly contract the disease in an area surrounding sites of infection. This required the training and subsequent dedicated work of many teams organised by the WHO, and a great deal of money and political will to implement. Since the vaccine is required in hot climates a heat-stable version had to be developed. This was done by freeze drying. A reliable distribution network for the vaccine also had to be set up. Despite all this, smallpox was *relatively* easy to eradicate compared with, say, malaria, partly because an effective vaccine was readily available and partly because the virus itself remained 'stable', not changing its antigens and thus not developing resistant strains. It was also easy to identify infected people, and the vaccine was easy to administer.

The smallpox story is also of interest because it was the first disease for which the principle of vaccination was applied. It was part of common folklore in the eighteenth century that an attack of cowpox gave protection from smallpox, cowpox being a mild disease often caught by milkmaids from cows with infected udders. In 1774, a Devonshire farmer named Benjamin Jesty, having become convinced of this by his own observations, created a local scandal by attempting to protect his wife and 2 children by scratching their arms with a needle and introducing material from sores on the udders of infected cows. (He had already had cowpox.) None of them ever caught smallpox. It was not until 1794, however, that Edward Jenner, a Gloucestershire country doctor, developed a scientific approach to the procedure. He extended the earlier discovery by inoculating a boy with cowpox and six weeks later inoculating him again with material from the skin of a smallpox victim. Fortunately, Jenner was proved correct in his belief that cowpox gave immunity to smallpox. The term vaccine derives from the name of the cowpox virus, *Vaccinia*, which in turn comes from the latin *vacca*, a cow. Smallpox vaccination was rapidly adopted in many countries and the number of epidemics began to decline. The modern vaccine contains a harmless strain of the vaccinia virus. As President Jefferson of the U.S.A. wrote to Jenner, 'Future nations will know by history only that the loathsome smallpox has existed and by you has been extirpated'.

5.9   Pros and cons of immunisation

Despite the huge advances in preventing epidemics of infectious diseases that have been made as a result of vaccination programmes, use of vaccines and antisera is not without its risks and has not taken place without a number of tragedies. Some of these have been the result of human error in preparing vaccines, particularly in the early days of vaccination. A few people who have defective immune systems are at risk from contracting the disease if a living vaccine is used, and there are occasional hypersensitive reactions to vaccination, though these are rarely lethal. A good example of this, and of the possible social consequences, is provided by the whooping cough vaccine. In the nineteenth and twentieth centuries whooping cough has been one of the most lethal of the common childhood diseases, killing more than a thousand children a year in Britain just before the vaccination programme was introduced in 1946. After that, incidence and severity of the disease fell dramatically (but see fig. 1.2 and section 1.3). In 1946 about 900 deaths occurred, with one death for every 70 cases notified. In 1955 there were about 100 deaths with one death for every 900 cases notified. Improved treatment of complications of the disease with antibiotics also contributed to the reduction in death rate. The trend continued, with about 19 000 cases notified in 1964 compared with 90 000 in 1955. No vaccine is 100% safe in all situations, and the whooping cough vaccine unfortunately causes convulsions in a few cases, and very rarely permanent brain damage (an estimated 1 in 100 000 vaccinations for the latter). During the 1970s, these dangers received widespread publicity and, since the disease had been reduced to such a low level, it was argued that there was now more risk from the vaccine than the disease. An interesting, and very real, moral dilemma thus arose for parents and doctors. Should parents nevertheless have their child vaccinated for the long-term benefit of the community, because as the number of children protected against the disease falls, so it becomes more common? The rate of vaccination against whooping cough fell from over 70% to about 30% of children and the consequence was a startling resurgence of the disease. In England and Wales in 1976 there were 4300 notified cases but from 1977 to 1979 a new epidemic struck, with

70 000 cases in 1978. More than 30 children died and others may suffer long-term brain damage. Epidemics tend to occur at regular intervals (another occurred in 1982 – see fig. 1.2). Another was anticipated to start in 1986 and a national advertising campaign was launched in that year to encourage parents to have children vaccinated. During the 1980s acceptance rates for vaccination have been going up again. Since even if the disease is not fatal, it can cause permanent brain or lung damage in more than 1% of cases, perhaps we should think in terms of protecting not only our children, but also our grandchildren by opting for vaccination. Routine vaccination is still recommended by the DHSS with the exception of those who are obviously at risk (see section 5.10). The vaccine is a suspension of dead *Bordetella pertussis* bacteria absorbed on aluminium salts. The cells contain the toxin. Protection requires the presence of *three* surface antigens. It is usually given in combination with diphtheria and tetanus toxoids. The schedule for vaccination is given in table 5.2.

Table 5.2 Recommended schedule of vaccination in Britain.

Age	Vaccine	Method
3 months (3 to 6 months)	DTP	injection
	polio	mouth
5 months (5 to 8 months)	DTP	injection
	polio	mouth
9 months (9 to 14 months)	DTP	injection
	polio	mouth
16 to 24 months	MMR**	injection
5 years (school entry)	DT (booster dose)	injection
	polio (booster dose)	mouth
10 to 13 years	BCG	injection
13 to 14 years, girls only	rubella* (German measles)	injection
16 to 18 years	tetanus (booster dose)	injection
	polio (booster dose)	mouth

DTP Diphtheria, tetanus and pertussis (whooping cough), known as 'triple vaccine'
      If pertussis is declined by parent or is contraindicated (likely to be unsafe), DT should
      be given.
DT Diphtheria, tetanus
BCG Tuberculosis vaccine
* Rubella vaccine is designed to protect women of child-bearing age because rubella may
cause damage to the foetus during pregnancy.
** MMR measles, mumps and rubella (German measles). A single injection for babies from
about 15 months. This will replace single measles and rubella injections.

5.10 Recommended schedule of vaccination

Table 5.2 shows the schedule of vaccination recommended by the DHSS. Vaccination should be avoided if the child is ill, or has ever had convulsions or if there is a history of convulsions in the family. Whooping cough vaccine should not be given to a child who has ever suffered epilepsy or any other disorder of the central nervous system.

5.11   Monoclonal antibodies

One of the most important advances in biotechnology to have been made in recent years is the development of monoclonal antibodies. The advance was pioneered by a British researcher, César Milstein, and a Swiss researcher, Georges Köhler, working in Cambridge in the late 1970s. They were awarded the Nobel Prize in 1984. Monoclonal means literally belonging to one clone. In this context, a clone is a group of genetically identical cells, all derived by growth and multiplication of one original parent cell. If the parent cell produced antibodies, then all members of a clone derived from the cell would produce identical antibodies. In this way large quantities of identical antibodies can be produced. As explained in section 5.4, antibodies are proteins and it would be impossible by conventional protein separation and purification techniques to obtain absolutely pure preparations of a given antibody from, say, a sample of blood. Until monoclonal antibodies became available, the main source of antibodies was blood serum from different species (see, for example, section 5.7). This contained antibodies against hundreds of substances. The method of deriving clones and the uses to which monoclonal antibodies can be put are described below.

Production of monoclonal antibodies

The aim is to produce an immortal lymphocyte that produces the correct antibody. The relevant antigen is injected into an experimental animal, usually a mouse, and time allowed for the antibodies to be made in response. Lymphocytes from the spleen or lymph nodes of the animal which are making the antibody are extracted and mixed in a culture with a particular type of cancer cell. Cell fusion is stimulated by adding polyethylene glycol (an anti-freeze agent!), with the result that some cells which are hybrids of lymphocytes and cancer cells will form in the culture. Conditions are arranged so that only hybrid cells will survive. Those that have retained the antibody-producing capacity of the original lymphocytes are selected and cloned, that is, single cells are introduced into culture solutions and allowed to grow and multiply, producing many identical daughter cells, all with the same antibody-producing capacity. Because the lymphocytes have been hybridised to cancer cells, they are immortal and can be grown in culture as a pure source of antibody indefinitely.

Uses of monoclonal antibodies

Each type of monoclonal antibody is specific for a particular antigen and will therefore 'home in' on the antigen and bind to it in a system containing the antigen. Monoclonal antibodies can therefore be used to identify antigens, find their precise locations and possibly to destroy the antigen. Applications include the following:

1   **Magic bullets and passive immunisation** If monoclonal antibodies to tumour antigens were combined with a toxic drug or a radioactive element, they could be used as 'magic bullets'. Injected into the body they would 'seek out' and attach specifically to the cancer cells of the tumour, and the attached drug or radioactive element would kill the

tumour cell without harming other parts of the body. This would be passive immunisation against cancer. The most recent research (1986) indicates that only small amounts of tumour will be able to be treated in this way. The magic bullets may therefore have a use in 'mopping up' the odd tumour cells that may remain in the body after surgery or radiotherapy.

Even if not coupled to another agent, monoclonal antibodies might be useful in attacking invading microorganisms such as the malaria parasite, HIV and other pathogens for which treatments are being sought.

2 **Diagnosis of disease and marker molecules** Monoclonal antibodies coupled to fluorescent molecules visible with a microscope can be used to identify locations of antigens, and hence the tissues or cells for which these antigens are specific. Diagnosis of *Chlamydia* is now possible using this technique, an important breakthrough given the previous difficulty in diagnosing the disease (see section 3.4). Early diagnosis of cancers may become possible, with greater possibilities of successful treatment. A similar technique has been used to screen for HIV and other pathogens.

As diagnostic tests become simpler, more are moving out of special- ised laboratories and into the doctor's surgery or even into the home. A monoclonal antibody-based test for streptococcal throat infections is a good recent example of this. The doctor can determine if a patient has a streptococcal infection immediately, and prescribe accordingly, with- out having to practise the defensive medicine necessary when labora- tory tests took several days.

3 **Tissue typing for transplants** Tissue typing, that is, determining the types of antigens present in a tissue to be used for transplant purposes, has traditionally been very difficult and not very accurate. Inaccurate tissue typing can lead to rejection of transplanted organs and the death of a patient. If, however, monoclonal antibodies are raised against the donor's antigens and then cross-matched with the recipient's anti- gens, the degree of binding will be a measure of the compatibility of the donor's tissue with the recipient's.

4 **Preventing rejection of transplants** A monoclonal antibody has been developed that may prevent rejection of kidney transplants. Rejection normally takes place when T cells of the immune system attack the new kidney. Monoclonal antibodies have been prepared which com- bine with and inactivate the T cells. The antibody has been developed by Britain's leading biotechnology company, Celltech, and will be the first monoclonal antibody to be used therapeutically.

5 **Monitoring spread of malaria** Monoclonal antibodies have been used to identify malarial sporozoites in infected mosquitoes. In this way the spread of malaria-carrying mosquitoes and the different types of malaria could be monitored, building up a better picture of the epidemiology of the disease.

6 Transplantation

6.1 Introduction

Transplantation is the replacement of damaged or diseased tissues or organs by healthy ones. The body reacts to transplants from another individual in the same way as it does to any other foreign material that possesses antigens, and makes antibodies against it. This leads to the phenomenon of **rejection** during which the foreign material is attacked by the body's immune system and eventually killed over a period of days or weeks. This problem must be overcome if the transplant is to be successful.

6.2 Types of transplant

Several types of transplant are possible:

autograft – tissue grafted from one part of the body to another part of the same body. Rejection not a problem. Used in skin grafting.

isograft – a graft between 2 genetically identical individuals, usually identical twins. Since antigens are determined genetically, grafts between genetically identical individuals are 'compatible' and unlikely to be rejected.

allograft – a graft between non-genetically identical individuals of the same species.

xenograft – a graft between individuals of different species, e.g. from pig to humans.

6.3 Rejection

Apart from skin grafting, transplant surgery is mainly concerned with allografts, although xenografting will probably become more common in the future. With blood transfusion (technically a tissue transplant) the immune problems are relatively easily overcome because the number of relevant antigens are few and well understood. A suitable ('compatible') donor is usually easy to find. A compatible donor is one who will not stimulate an immune response in the recipient. Apart from the ABO system of blood group antigens, which induce a strong response in recipients, there is another dominant group of antigens in humans which makes transplantation particularly difficult. These are coded for by genes on chromosome 6 which together are described as the **major histocompatibility complex (MHC)** or **human lymphocyte antigen** group (HLA) in humans. Several hundred proteins, concerned with many aspects of the immune response, are coded for by this group of genes, so 'tissue matching' individuals for the purposes of transplantation becomes a formidable task, and only partial matching is possible, unless identical twins are used. The more closely related the individuals, the closer their genetic resemblance and likelihood of sharing similar antigens. Ideally, long-term tissue and organ storage banks, and international cooperation, are required to make the best use of graft material as it becomes available. At present, however, techniques for long-term organ storage are inadequate.

Prevention of graft rejection

There are several methods currently available to minimise graft rejection.

1 **Tissue matching** – as close a match as possible. Close relatives, particularly brothers, sisters, parents and children are best. The aim is to minimise differences in major antigens between donor and recipient.

2 **Immunosuppressive drugs** – chemicals which inhibit activity of the immune system, so rejection cannot take place. A major problem is that the patient becomes susceptible to all kinds of infection and is at great risk even from normally minor infections. Growth of tumours, damage to bones and body organs may also occur. Treatment must continue for the rest of the patient's life.

3 **X-ray radiation of the bone marrow and lymphoid tissues** – inhibits blood cell production and therefore slows down rejection. Unpleasant side effects and greater susceptibility to infection occur.

4 **Suppression of T cell activity** – rejection has been shown to be caused mainly by cell-mediated immunity, i.e. by T cells. In the future, a more specific immunosuppression of T cells may allow the rest of the patient's immune system (B cells) to function unimpaired. One possibility is to use monoclonal antibodies which recognise and destroy T cells (see section 5.11).

The protective measures described under 2 to 4 above all carry great risks and can be very restrictive on the lifestyles of transplant patients and their families. An extended period of convalescence in a germ-free hospital environment may be necessary. Regular pill-taking, susceptibility to minor illness and possibly very gradual long-term rejection are all restrictions on a normal life. Since the alternative is usually death or painful and debilitating illness, the transplant option is often to be preferred.

6.4 Kidney transplants

Kidneys are the most commonly transplanted organs. About 1500 a year are currently transplanted in Britain, although the average waiting list is 3500 to 4000 people (70 per million of the population). There is a high survival rate. Some recipients of kidney transplants have lived for 15 years or more with the transplanted organ. There are two important reasons for this success. Firstly, each person has two kidneys and since it is possible to survive with one kidney, close relatives (ideally an identical twin) are sometimes willing to donate a kidney. In such situations tissue matching is much closer than usual and rejection is less likely. Matching of tissue types is now done by computer. In Holland, a computer system called Eurotransplant operates which enables suitable kidneys to be exchanged between countries. Speed and efficiency is essential because the kidney must be removed within 30 minutes after the donor's death and transplanted within 24 hours.

A second reason for the success of kidney transplants is that failure of the transplanted organ does not necessarily lead to death. This is because the patient can be kept alive on an artificial kidney machine until another transplant becomes available. With the artificial kidney machine, blood is removed from the body and circulated through the machine for dialysis (filtration) before returning to the body. Although dialysis can be carried out in the home, it must be done every few days and the machines, supporting staff and resources to run them, are very expensive. Currently it costs about £15 000 per year per patient. This raises ethical problems about how much money should be spent on the machines and who should be selected to use them when demand exceeds supply.

Many of those waiting for kidney transplants are children who have been ill since they were babies, and whose growth has been slow as a result of their condition. More kidney donors are needed to cope with this demand. Alternatively use may be made of xenografts from animals such as pigs or sheep once rejection problems are overcome. The pig has been described as a 'horizontal human' because it is comparable in size and weight to humans.

6.5 Heart transplants

With organs other than the kidney, transplantation is not normally recommended unless it is the only alternative to early death. Close matching of organs is, therefore, sometimes difficult due to urgency. Heart transplants have excited much greater public interest than any other transplants because there is something uniquely emotive about the heart as an organ. Despite this, the heart is a very simple organ and the techniques involved in heart surgery are in essence very straightforward. The demand for heart transplantation is high, with an estimated 400 people per million in the population needing a heart or heart/lung transplant.

The first heart transplant was carried out in Capetown in 1967 by Dr Christian Barnard. In Britain, Papworth Hospital and Harefield Hospital have been among the pioneers. During the operation the patient is kept alive on a heart–lung machine which takes over the role of circulating and oxygenating the blood. The major medical problem is again that of rejection, although drugs such as cyclosporine now help prevent early rejection. Few recipients of new hearts live longer than 5 years after the operation. About half survive for at least one year. This is longer than they might have expected without the operation and the quality of life is usually much improved, with relief from pain, fatigue and breathlessness. Because of the problems, relatively few heart transplants are carried out. Future progress is likely to involve the use of artificial hearts or xenografts from animals such as cattle, sheep or, most likely, pigs. Pigs are already extensively used as a source of heart valves. Baboons and chimpanzees have been tried without success. Development of an artificial polyurethane heart has been underway since 1974. Four had been implanted in the U.S.A. and one in Europe by March 1986. The latter was used for 24 hours only until a donated heart could be supplied.

6.6 Social and moral implications of transplantation

A number of social and moral problems associated with transplantation, and worthy of discussion, have been identified in the previous sections and are outlined below:

    1 Transplantation surgery is relatively expensive (see sections 6.4 and 6.5). Given the problems, can this expense be justified when the

demands of less glamorous areas of medicine are considered? A kidney transplant may cost £20 000. On the other hand £100 million a year is being spent on kidney dialysis.

2 In the case of kidney transplants, is it ethical to ask close relatives to donate kidneys, thus putting them under moral pressure to agree, despite the fact that there must be some degree of risk to their own lives?

3 Transplantation requires a steady supply of suitable donors. This raises questions about how donors should be selected. Since organs are required in perfect condition they must be removed from donors as soon as the latter are pronounced clinically dead. It can be stressful to close relatives to be asked permission in these circumstances. Donor cards carried by individuals willing to donate their organs after death are an obvious solution to this problem, although care must be exercised to ensure that persons found to be antibody-positive for HIV do not carry donor cards.

4 There has been concern that the criteria for clinical death may not be applied as rigorously as they should. For example, should a brain scan, whose purpose is to detect any remaining electrical activity in the brain, be routinely applied?

5 How do we select who should *receive* donated organs when only a limited number are available? In the future, more use will probably be made of animals as donors (see sections 6.4 and 6.5). Is this morally justifiable? Some Animal Rights campaigners have already described such prospects as a 'gross abuse of animal life' and a 'sick horror fantasy'. Animals used would be operated on under anaesthetic and then humanely killed. We already slaughter 400 million animals a year for food.

6 Possibility of failure is high. Is it right to raise people's hopes, even if risks are explained?

7 Transplant patients must undergo risky and demanding immuno-suppressive treatment (see section 6.3).

7 Pulmonary diseases

7.1 Introduction

The term **pulmonary** refers to the lungs. They form part of the respiratory system whose function is to supply oxygen to the blood and to remove carbon dioxide. The lungs and respiratory pathway are a major route of entry to the body and as such are a common target of infectious agents and toxic (noxious) materials from the environment, particularly the work environment. Both these forms of attack are considered in this chapter. Infectious diseases include influenza (section 2.1), pulmonary TB (section 2.5), common cold and pneumonia. Maintaining healthy lungs is not simply a question of avoiding disease and noxious agents, but of being aware of the positive contributions which the individual can make to his or her own well-being. In testing the efficiency of the lungs the functions of ventilation (breathing) and gas exchange (relative proportions of oxygen and carbon dioxide in inspired and expired air) can easily be checked and monitored (see section 9.5).

7.2 Survey of occupational lung disorders

Over 80% of the noxious agents found in industry gain access to the body through the lungs. The harmful effects produced by noxious agents can be grouped as follows:

1 **Acute inflammation** Caused by irritant gases and fumes such as ammonia, chlorine, sulpur dioxide, nitrogen oxides and ozone.
2 **Asthma** This may be caused by an allergic response to dust from a variety of materials, often of organic/biological origin. Up to 15% of all asthmas could be occupationally related. Constriction of the air pathways occurs by uncontrollable contractions of smooth muscle.
3 **Byssinosis** Flow of air into and out of the lungs is impeded in an asthma-like response. It is induced by exposure to dusts of cotton, sisal, hemp or flax.
4 **Pneumoconiosis** The term literally means 'dusty lungs'. It refers to permanent lung damage caused by inhalation of mineral dusts, chiefly coal, silica (causing **silicosis**) and asbestos (causing **asbestosis**). These are dealt with in section 7.5.
5 **Alveolitis** This is a reduction in transfer of gases between the alveoli and blood caused by an allergic response to some organic dusts. It is mostly caused by fungal spores. The most common condition in Britain is **farmer's lung** caused by spores of mould fungi which are found in hay. More exotic conditions include **bird fancier's lung**, **cheese worker's lung** and **animal handler's lung**. Acute influenze-like symptoms occur with **fibrosis** of the lung (build up of non-elastic white fibres).
6 **Lung cancer** See section 7.6.

7.3 Structure of the gas exchange organs

In order to understand the effects of pulmonary diseases, some knowledge of the normal healthy structure of the lungs, including some of their detailed histology (tissue structure) is required. This is dealt with in standard 'A' level biology texts.

7.4 Emphysema and bronchitis

Emphysema describes a condition in which the walls of the alveoli lose their elasticity and break down, reducing the surface area for gas exchange. It usually arises after prolonged disease of the lung and is untreatable once firmly established. It occurs when the alveoli are constantly subjected to higher than normal pressure and become over-inflated and over-stretched. This may occur if the air pathways into the lungs become narrower, resulting in difficulty in breathing and shortness of breath (*dyspnoea*). Asthma and chronic bronchitis are the chief causes of this. The physical stress of coughing, extra force of inspiration and possible bacterial damage in some diseases all contribute to the damage.

About 1 person in 100 in Britain suffers to some extent from emphysema and it is 10 times more common in men than women. Smoking and air pollution dramatically increase the risks (see sections 7.7 and 7.8). Shortness of breath occurs (though coughing is *not* a sign of *emphysema*). The loss of elasticity of the lungs results in a loss of involuntary expiration; in other words, the victim must make a conscious effort to breathe out. The victim is more prone to lung infections, and oxygen shortage puts a strain on the cardiovascular system as it tries to compensate. The right side of the heart particularly is strained since the blood it pumps to the lungs cannot flow freely through the capillaries. This leads to heart failure (inefficient pumping). Blood backs up in the veins leading to the heart, and fluid accumulates in the tissues, notably the legs and ankles.

Bronchitis is inflammation of the air passages and may be acute or **chronic**. Chronic refers to an illness that persists for many years and may start with minor signs and symptoms that get worse. Note that bronchitis is *not* an infectious disease. Like emphysema it is caused by smoking or air pollution. Children of heavy smokers may be affected. Acute bronchitis usually lasts only a few days as a result, for example, of a cold, and generally causes no long-term damage. Chronic bronchitis, however, *kills* about 30 000 people a year in Britain (1 person in 2000, the highest rate in the world) and about one million others are affected. Three times as many men as women are affected.

The characteristic sign is a cough, often starting as a morning cough, that brings up sputum (phlegm). Extra mucus is produced as a result of the inflammation. Later the cilia may be lost as the lining of the bronchi is damaged and coughing is then the only way in which the mucus can be got rid of. Long term, infection causes narrowing of the bronchi due to thickening and scarring of their walls and contraction of the smooth muscle, as well as emphysema (see above). Coughing, breathlessness and wheezing occur throughout the day, and the amount of sputum produced gradually increases as the disease progresses. The most effective treatment is usually to avoid smoking. Colds and flu bring on dangerously acute attacks. Increased susceptibility to diseases like pneumonia occurs.

7.5 Pneumoconiosis

Pneumoconiosis ('dusty lungs') is a common industrial disease caused, as explained in section 7.2, by inhalation of various mineral dusts, usually over many years. Table 7.1 summarises the causes and effects of the different types.

Table 7.1 Causes and effects of different types of pneumoconiosis.

Type of pneumoconiosis	Cause	People most at risk	Effects on health
Simple	carbon particles (soot in smoke)	city dwellers	dirty lungs, not usually very harmful
Silicosis	silica (quartz) particles	sandblasters, glass workers, stone masons, quarry and mine-workers	extensive fibrosis* and lung damage Makes pulmonary T.B. more serious
Coal-miner's pneumoconiosis	coal dust	coal miners	fibrosis* (no longer common since dust levels in mines reduced)
Asbestosis	asbestos fibres (blue asbestos far more dangerous than white asbestos)	building and construction workers	Extensive fibrosis* commonly fatal, lung cancer a frequent complication, especially with blue asbestos

*Fibrosis: increase in amount of non-elastic fibres (collagen) in walls of alveoli. Reduces elasticity and hence efficiency of gas exchange.

7.6 Lung cancer

Cancer is caused when cells are induced to divide and multiply out of control. In effect they lose their sense of identity, and cease to respond to the normal limiting factors in the tissues around them. They usually become unspecialised (undifferentiated) cells, forming masses called **tumours**. A tumour that continues to spread is termed **malignant**. Any agent which induces cancer is termed a **carcinogen** and is described as **carcinogenic**. These agents include certain types of radiation such as ultra-violet light and ionising radiations like X-rays and gamma-rays. They also include a vast array of chemical substances. Often several factors combine to cause cancer. There are several types of lung cancer, but by far the most common (99% of cases) is **bronchial carcinoma**. (A carcinoma is a cancer arising in epithelia.) At one time this was a rare disease, but during the twentieth century it has increased in incidence as a result of tobacco smoking (see section 7.7) to the point where it is a leading cause of death in some industrialised countries. It is the most common form of cancer in the western world and is most common in Britain, where it causes 1 in 18 deaths. The disease starts with a few damaged cells which develop into a tumour that spreads into the lungs. Tumour cells may also spread into the bloodstream and cause secondary cancers in other parts of the body.

Only 0.3% of those who die from the disease are life-long non-smokers. More men than women die from the disease, though the numbers of men dying are now declining while those of women are rising, another factor attributable to patterns of smoking. In the mid-1950s 10 times more men than women died of lung cancer compared with 3 times more men in 1983. In women, lung cancer is beginning to overtake breast cancer as the commonest form of cancer.

The first sign of lung cancer is a cough, more persistent than the usual smoker's cough, accompanied by chest pain and sputum which may be blood-stained. Weight loss and appetite loss may occur. Early diagnosis is possible by X-ray, and routine screening by chest radiography is therefore advisable. Surgical removal of the tumour at an early stage often effects a cure.

7.7 Effects of tobacco smoke on the gas exchange system

It has already been noted that tobacco smoke can cause lung cancer, but it also has other ill effects on the lungs and other parts of the body. This is not surprising considering the complex mixture of noxious chemicals in tobacco smoke, the delicacy of lung tissue and the direct access the lungs provide to the rest of the body via the blood. The effects of tobacco smoke on the cardiovascular system will be considered further in chapter 8.

It is important to realise that tobacco smoke is a *mixture* of chemicals, in particulate form, gas or solution, and that a scientific approach to a study of its effects must involve an evaluation of the contribution of each of its constituents. In addition, investigations are complicated by 2 further considerations:

1 The constituents of tobacco smoke, particularly the carcinogens, may interact synergistically with each other. In other words, their combined effects are multiplied and much greater than the sum of their effects in isolation.

2 Factors such as air pollution, climate, occupation and age, may also influence the response of the body.

With respect to the second point, it is therefore important to include suitable control groups wherever possible when carrying out epidemiological work so that one can evaluate the effects of tobacco smoke in isolation from other factors. As with other scientific data, any statistics should be studied carefully with regard to sample sizes, controls and variables. It is also important to distinguish between correlation and causation. A correlation between, say, lung cancer and cigarette smoking does not in itself prove that smoking causes lung cancer. However, if the chemicals in tobacco smoke cause cancer in laboratory animals, then a causal relationship looks likely.

Since the early 1970s the total number of smokers has declined among men and women (can you explain why the number of deaths from lung cancer among women is still rising? – see Smoking and lung cancer below). During this period smoking has increasingly become regarded as an anti-social habit (see fig. 7.1).

Tobacco is thought to account for 15–20% of all British deaths (around 100 000 people per year). The 3 main diseases closely linked with smoking are coronary heart disease, lung cancer and chronic bronchitis. Other smoking-related diseases include emphysema; mouth, throat, pancreas and bladder cancer; narrowing of blood vessels in the limbs (leading in severe cases to amputation); other cardiovascular disease and peptic ulcers. The unborn child is also affected if the mother smokes.

Sickness due to smoking results in an estimated loss of 50 million working days each year with a consequent drain on the National Health Service, estimated to be £155 million in 1981.

The 3 constituents of tobacco smoke which probably do most harm are nicotine, carbon monoxide and tar. The levels of these have all been reduced in cigarettes over the last 20 years.

Nicotine

Nicotine is a drug which is quickly absorbed by the blood if smoke is inhaled. It may reach the brain in less than 30 seconds. Its concentration in the blood rises steeply during smoking. Nicotine stimulates the sympathetic nervous system and release of adrenaline, thus increasing heart rate and blood pressure. The latter may damage blood capillaries in the lungs, particularly if a person is already suffering lung damage such as emphysema. Similarly, in some circumstances, extra strain on the heart and peripheral blood vessels may prove harmful, as in a patient with heart disease. Nicotine also increases the stickiness of blood platelets, a factor which may cause blood clotting.

The pleasure of smoking derives largely, though not exclusively, from the effects of nicotine. Its effects on behaviour are complex and vary between individuals. It makes the smoker feel more relaxed and capable of facing stressful situations, and it increases arousal in some situations, as when performing boring tasks. These facts have to be borne in mind if attempts are made to give up smoking because, for example, alternative ways of relieving stress may have to be found.

Carbon monoxide

Up to 5% of cigarette smoke is carbon monoxide, a toxic gas. Carbon monoxide combines irreversibly with haemoglobin in the red blood cells to form carboxyhaemoglobin. Thus it lowers the oxygen-carrying capacity of the blood. Regular smokers commonly have a 3 to 7% permanent reduction in capacity.

The health consequences of this are not clear, although it would be reasonable to assume that it is potentially harmful in situations where oxygen supply becomes critical, notably in coronary heart disease or asthma. Recent evidence suggests that it aggravates angina. It also seems to slow growth of the foetus, which may be born prematurely and/or underweight.

Tars

Tobacco tar is an irritant. It enters the respiratory pathway as an aerosol of invisibly minute droplets, about 70% of which are deposited in the respiratory pathway if the smoke is inhaled. The irritation causes chronic inflammation of the lining ('mucous membrane') of the pathway, causing thickening of the epithelium and appearance of scar tissue in the long-term. Tar is the chief cause of the chronic bronchitis which typically affects smokers, and whose signs and symptoms have been described in section 7.4.

It destroys or paralyses cilia of the respiratory tract and thus inhibits the wafting of mucus up to the back of the throat. Mucus, together with its trapped dust and germs, therefore slides down into the lungs, increasing the risk of infection and damage. Tar causes extra secretion of mucus from goblet cells.

Tars also contain carcinogens which, combined with the physical degeneration of the mucous membranes, greatly increases the chances of developing lung cancer (see section 7.6). The same chemicals can be shown to induce cancers in laboratory animals. Light smokers are 10 times more likely to get lung cancer than non-smokers, and heavy smokers 25 times. 'Passive smoking', that is, being in a smoky environment even if not a smoker oneself, also increases the risks. Cancers of the mouth and throat are also possible since some smoke is swallowed. The dangers start to decline as soon as smoking ceases.

Since tars are regarded as the single most dangerous constituent of cigarette smoke, cigarettes are classified as low tar (0 to 10 mg/cigarette) through to high tar (29 + mg/cig), and there has been greater encouragement to smoke low tar brands.

Irritants

Irritants other than tars exist in tobacco smoke, and add to the irritant effects of tars described above.

Smoking and lung cancer

A description of lung cancer has been given in section 7.6. The first indications that cigarette smoking was harmful came with the ten-fold rise in lung cancer deaths among men between 1900 and 1945. An investigation of this established a correlation with smoking. In a classic follow-up study advantage was taken of the fact that large numbers of doctors subsequently gave up smoking, the proportion halving from 43% to 21% between 1954 and 1971. At the same time, the proportion of all men smoking remained about the same. During this period, death rate from lung cancer fell by 25% in doctors while increasing in the general population by 26%. There has been a recent decline in lung cancer among men, though it is still rising among women, (fig. 7.2) probably the delayed effect of their increased cigarette consumption from the Second World War on, when it became much more socially acceptable for women to smoke (fig. 7.1). By 1945 cigarette smoking among males had peaked and even dropped before settling to a fairly constant level (fig. 7.1). The recent downward trend in lung cancer mortality among British males may be due to reductions in tar and nicotine content of cigarettes. The data in table 7.2 support this view.

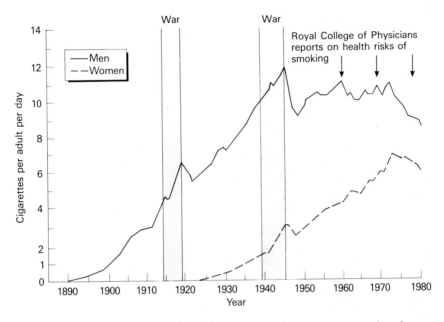

Figure 7.1 Tobacco consumption in the UK 1890 to 1981, given as average number of cigarettes per adult per day for men and women separately, irrespective of whether they smoke or not, from *Health or Smoking?* Royal College of Physicians Pitman (1983)

Table 7.2 Changes in England and Wales in male lung cancer death rates in early middle age since tar deliveries have been reduced. (From Table 3.1 *Health or smoking?* Roy. Coll. of Physicians, Pitman, 1983.)

Age at time of observation	Death rates per million men from cancers of the respiratory tract, excluding larynx		
	Men born in about 1910, and observed in 1940–1960	Men born in about 1930–1950, and observed in 1980	Ratio
30–34	39**	13	0.3
35–39	98**	45	0.5
40–44	253**	134	0.5
45–49	597**	378*	0.6

* High mean tar intake only in first decade or so of smoking history.
** High mean tar intake throughout smoking history.

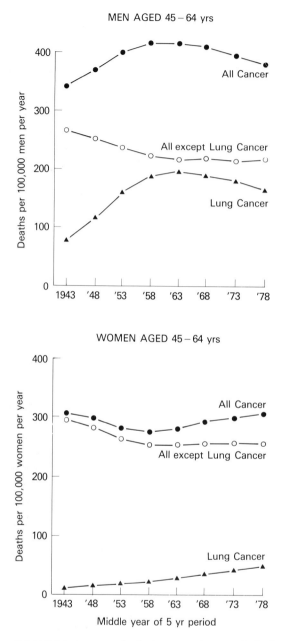

Figure 7.2 Lung cancer deaths in men and women in England and Wales, data from *Health or Smoking?* Royal College of Physicians Pitman (1983)

Smoking and chronic lung disease

Cigarette smoking appears to be the dominant cause of chronic bronchitis, the death rate being 6 times greater among smokers than non-smokers (25 times greater if smoking more than 25 cigarettes per day). Characteristics of chronic bronchitis are given in section 7.4.

8 Cardiovascular diseases

8.1 Introduction, and incidence of cardiovascular disease

The cardiovascular system comprises the heart and blood vessels, and has the vital function of circulating the blood. Every 3 to 4 minutes someone in Britain dies of cardiovascular disease. It is Britain's biggest killer, accounting for 44% of all premature deaths (twice as many as cancer). This represents nearly 140 000 people per year under the age of 75, and is one of the highest rates in the world (see fig. 8.1). It is also the most expensive illness in this country, resulting in more than 65 million lost working days each year, and a heavy demand on the resources of the NHS. Apart from the high mortality rate, *chronic* heart disease causes incapacitation, suffering and pain in many of its victims. Much heart disease is self-inflicted and therefore avoidable, as will become clear.

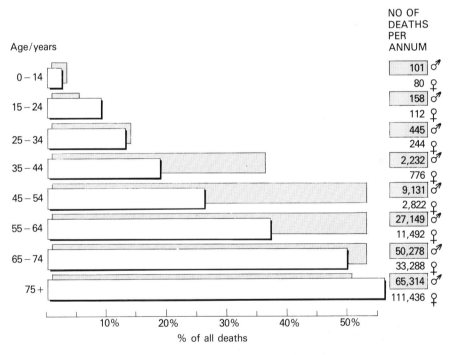

Figure 8.1 Deaths from heart and circulatory diseases as a % of all deaths, Britain 1983. Source: British Heart Foundation, citing Office of Population Censuses and Surveys and Registrar General for Scotland

The relative importance of different types of cardiovascular disease is shown in fig. 8.2, the legend of which explains some of the terms used in describing the diseases. It will be seen that coronary heart disease is the biggest single killer, accounting for about two thirds of fatalities. During 1980, coronary heart disease accounted for 31% of *all* deaths of men in England and Wales (more than 3 times the number for lung cancer). With a 5-fold increase since the

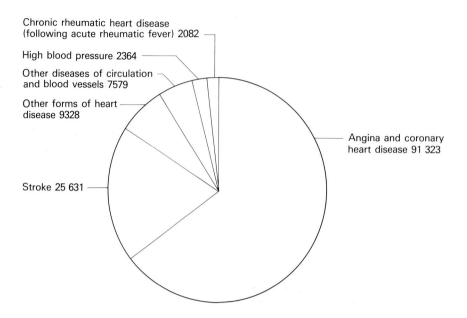

Chronic rheumatic heart disease
(following acute rheumatic fever) 2082

High blood pressure 2364

Other diseases of circulation
and blood vessels 7579

Other forms of heart
disease 9328

Stroke 25 631

Angina and coronary
heart disease 91 323

Figure 8.2 Deaths due to heart and circulatory diseases under age 74, Britain 1983. Source: British Heart Foundation, citing Office of Population Censuses and Surveys and Registrar General for Scotland. *Rheumatic fever:* an acute illness most commonly occurring in children and adolescents; connective tissues become inflamed, particularly in joints and in the lining and valves of the heart, the heart may be permanently damaged, eventually leading to heart failure and 'chronic rheumatic heart disease' (late complications)

Second World War, it has been called the 'modern epidemic', being as important in scale as some of the infectious diseases of the past. Strokes account for about one fifth of deaths; they are the third most common cause of death in the western world (after heart disease and cancer) and the single most common cause of disability. Coronary heart disease and strokes are the two diseases on which we shall be focusing our attention in this chapter.

Note, however, that research into heart disease involves more than just attempts to prevent and treat these 2 major killers. Other forms of heart disease occur; for example, more than 1000 children die every year in Britain from heart defects.

Note also that a distinction must be made between cardiovascular disease (which includes strokes, for example) and heart disease (which does not include strokes).

8.2 Normal structure and function of the heart

A knowledge of the normal structure and functioning of the cardiovascular system is necessary to understand the diseases that may affect it. Standard texts cover the structure of the system and the mechanisms controlling the 'cardiac cycle' (heartbeat). The structure of the heart can only be fully appreciated by means of dissection, and it is recommended that such a dissection is carried out (see, for example, *UCLES* 'A' level Biology Paper 5, 1987).

8.3 Atherosclerosis and arteriosclerosis

The underlying cause of coronary heart disease, strokes and other diseases affecting the blood vessels, is usually **atherosclerosis**. During this process, fatty substances, some blood products and a high proportion of cholesterol* are deposited within the inner coat of the arteries, usually the large arteries. Arterioles and other blood vessels are largely unaffected. The deposit is called **atheroma** and causes the arterial walls to thicken, and hence the lumen to narrow. It starts as fatty streaks that usually develop into uneven patches called **plaques**, or **atheromatous plaques**. Fatty streaks often start to appear in childhood, and atheromatous plaques are found in the arteries of virtually all young adults. The plaques take many years to reach the stage where health is affected. Figure 8.3 shows stages in the process.

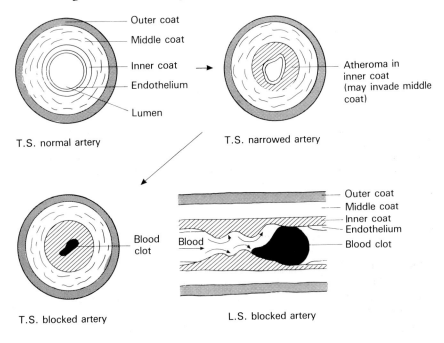

Figure 8.3 The process of atherosclerosis

 atheroma

The onset of an atheromatous plaque may be caused by some physical damage to the lining of the artery, perhaps by the high arterial pressure. Smooth muscle cells proliferate at the site of damage and then lipids and cholesterol are deposited from the blood. The presence of atheromatous plaques roughens the lining of the artery and disturbs the otherwise smooth flow of blood.

*Cholesterol belongs to a group of chemicals known as steroids, which are related to lipids (fats and oils). It is an essential constituent of the diet since it is involved in the manufacture of other steroids such as cholic acid (used to make bile salts) and the sex hormones. Excess, however, is probably harmful as explained in the text.

It is believed that this roughness can stimulate the slow development of a blood clot over the plaque (see fig. 8.3). An abnormal clot that develops in a blood vessel is called a **thrombus**. If the clot breaks away from its attachment to the wall due to the flow of blood, it is called an **embolus**. This can travel through the blood vessels and jam at any narrow point in the system, causing cessation or restriction of blood flow to the affected area.

Atherosclerosis may be associated with another process, known as **arterio-sclerosis**, which also takes a long time to develop and which is associated with ageing. In arteriosclerosis, fibrous deposits are laid down in the damaged areas (**fibrosis**) and calcium is also often deposited, giving rise to **calcified** plaques. Fibrosis and calcification cause the artery wall to harden and cease to be elastic. Arteriosclerosis is sometimes known simply as 'hardening of the arteries'. Such arteries are prone to rupture and are also liable to initiate development of a thrombus, particularly if the atheroma breaks through the endothelium of the blood vessel.

Possible underlying causes of atherosclerosis and cardiovascular disease

Little is known about the underlying causes of atherosclerosis despite intensive research and the study of entire populations of many different countries. Results show that there is no single cause, but that several different factors combine together. Three factors that are clearly associated with the condition are damage to the artery wall, high blood cholesterol levels and genetic predisposition to the disease. Atherosclerosis is often described as a disease of old age, but as noted already it takes many years to develop and it is not an inevitable consequence of ageing. It is far more common among men than women (up to five times as common), particularly in age groups below 50 years. This may be related to sex hormones, since there is evidence that the female sex hormones can have a protective effect. This protection disappears at menopause.

Severe diabetes and severe hypothyroidism frequently lead to atherosclerosis, both diseases being associated with high blood cholesterol levels. Hypertension (high blood pressure) doubles the risk, possibly as a result of pressure damage to arteries. Finally, people who have a diet rich in saturated fats or cholesterol have been shown to be at far greater risk of developing atherosclerosis.

Risk factors for atherosclerosis and cardiovascular disease

Whatever the underlying causes of atherosclerosis and cardiovascular disease, a number of risk factors are known to be important. The three *most* important are diet, raised blood pressure and smoking. These are considered below. Another contributory factor, lack of exercise, is considered in chapter 9. The risk factors interact (see risk assessment test, table 8.1 and section 8.4). Some of them are avoidable, particularly smoking, poor diet and lack of exercise and greater public awareness of these is therefore desirable.

Diet and cardiovascular disease (CV disease)

One factor which is believed to be particularly likely to increase the risk of cardiovascular disease is the excessive consumption of saturated fats and cholesterol. Another diet-related problem, obesity, imposes an extra strain on the cardiovascular system, but is discussed in more detail in another book in this series, *Human nutrition* (Walker).

In countries such as Greece and Japan, where heart disease is relatively rare, lower fat intakes and lower blood cholesterol levels are found than is typical of people in Britain. Figure 8.4 shows the wide variation that exists in death rates from **coronary heart disease** in different countries.

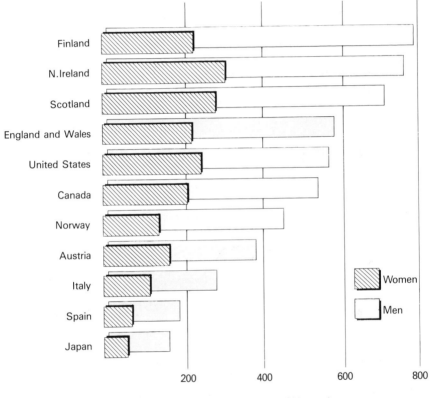

Figure 8.4 Death rates from coronary heart disease in different countries (35–74 year olds), from *Beating Heart Disease* Health Education Council

The amount of cholesterol in the blood seems to be mainly influenced by the amount of saturated fats, rather than the amount of cholesterol, in the diet. A summary of the meanings of some of the terms associated with fats is given below since it is important in understanding the effects of fats on health:

A lipid which is *solid* at room temperature (20°C) is a *fat*.
A lipid which is *liquid* at room temperature (20°C) is an *oil*.
Saturated fats or fatty acids – molecules have no double bonds (saturated with hydrogen).
Unsaturated fats or fatty acids – molecules have double bonds (unsaturated with

hydrogen). Unsaturated fats may be mono- or polyunsaturated:

Monounsaturated one double bond, e.g. oleic acid.

Polyunsaturated – more than one double bond, e.g. linoleic acid. Two of the three common polyunsaturated fatty acids are essential fatty acids.

Fats made up predominantly of unsaturated fatty acids are called *unsaturated fats*. Fats made up predominantly of saturated fatty acids are called *saturated fats*. The more saturated a fat, the more solid it is (higher the melting point). Vegetable oils are most commonly liquid polyunsaturated fats. The ratio of polyunsaturated fatty acid (PUFA) to saturated fatty acid in the diet has an important influence on levels of blood cholesterol. Saturated fatty acids raise blood cholesterol; PUFAs *lower* blood cholesterol. Monounsaturated fatty acids have no effect.

Hydrogenated fatty acids/fats – oils can be hardened to make margarines by converting a high proportion of their unsaturated fatty acids to saturated fatty acids. This is done by adding hydrogen (hydrogenation).

'Cis' and 'Trans' fatty acids – most natural unsaturated fatty acids are in the *cis* form where the molecules are fairly straight. When unsaturated fatty acids are hydrogenated (see above) some of the remaining unsaturated fatty acids are converted into the *trans* form in which the molecules have kinks. These have the same effects on our bodies as saturated fatty acids. New labelling regulations may require minimum levels of *cis* fatty acids to be specified on the labels of polyunsaturated margarines and oils.

Saturated fats are typically animal fats. They are solid at normal room temperatures and include butter and lard. Unsaturated fats are typically plant fats and are soft at room temperature, or liquid (oils), e.g. olive oil, sunflower oil. Margarines are usually (not always – check the label!) high in polyunsaturated fats. Figure 8.5 shows the fat composition of various foods and could be used to help plan a diet lower in saturated fats. It should perhaps be noted that while milk products such as cream and cheese are rich in fat (e.g. cheddar cheese 34% fat, double cream 50% fat), milk itself is only 3 to 4% fat (skimmed milk less than 1%).

The World Health Organisation recommended in 1982 that people in Britain should cut the amount of saturated fat eaten by half and increase the amount of polyunsaturated fat eaten. Two further important documents of recent years have been the NACNE report (National Advisory Committee on Nutrition Education) in 1983 and the COMA report (Committee On Medical Aspects of Food Policy) in 1984 on 'Diet and Cardiovascular Disease'. It admits that the evidence linking CV disease with diet 'falls short of proof' and that the relationship between the two is complex, but recommends changes in the diet which it believes are likely to lead to health benefits.

JACNE (the Joint Advisory Committee on Nutrition Education) replaced NACNE in 1984 with a brief to turn the COMA report into a practical guide for the public.

The importance of diet is still not fully understood or agreed among the experts but there have been some general agreements, and all have recommended similar changes in diet. COMA's recommendations for the U.K. include:

1 National average intake of fat should be reduced from the present level of 40% of total food energy to 35%. (NACNE recommends a target of

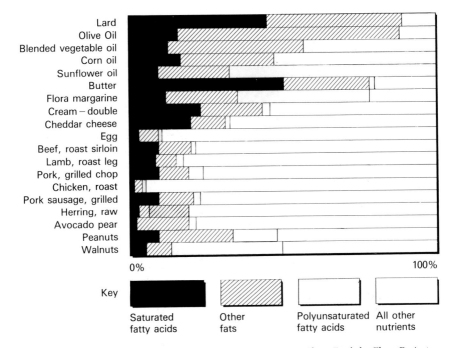

Figure 8.5 Fat composition of different foods, from 'Finding Out About Fats' the Flora Project for Heart Disease Prevention

30%). This represent a 17% ($\frac{1}{6}$) reduction in fat content of the diet.

2 A maximum of 15% of food energy should come from saturated fatty acids. Average consumption of saturated fatty acids should be decreased by 25%. (Experiments in the 1970s showed that cutting down on saturated fatty acids in the diet and replacing them with polyunsaturated fatty acids reduced cholesterol levels.)

High blood pressure (hypertension) and cardiovascular disease

High blood pressure (**hypertension**) is a common problem from middle age onwards. It is often symptomless, but places an extra burden on the heart, making it work harder, speeds up development of atheroma, and increases the danger of suffering angina, a heart attack or stroke. High blood pressure may be induced by being overweight, smoking, drinking excessive alcohol, lack of regular exercise, too much stress and possibly too much salt in the diet, although there is controversy over how these factors operate. Regular checks of blood pressure by general practitioners are advisable from middle age. Probably less than half the GPs in Britain operate such systematic screening, compared with probably more than two thirds in the U.S.A., where there is greater public attention to cardiovascular fitness. Normal blood pressure is about 120 mm mercury (16 kPa) systolic over 80 mm mercury (10.7 kPa) diastolic for a healthy young adult (120/80). A diastolic of more than 100 (13.3 kPa) gives cause for concern and more than 130 (17.3 kPa) is serious. Average blood pressure tends to increase with age. The average diastolic pressure of a 70 year old is about 90 (12 kPa).

Smoking and cardiovascular disease

The harmful effects of smoking on the respiratory system have already been considered in chapter 7. However, CV disease accounts for more than one third of the excess deaths due to smoking, with the greatest increases being for coronary heart disease. For example, a man of 50 who smokes more than 20 cigarettes a day is four times more likely to suffer from heart disease than a non-smoker of the same age. Smoking has been shown to be particularly associated with deposition of fatty plaques in blood vessels (atherosclerosis) and narrowing of arteries. It also causes a reduction in the ability to remove blood clots and a reduction in the heart's oxygen supply. Narrowing of the carotid arteries, which supply the brain, may cause strokes. A further complication associated with smoking is atherosclerosis of the peripheral arteries supplying the legs (**peripheral vascular disease**). This causes pain, often crippling pain, on walking and may lead to death of tissues, subsequent gangrene and the need for amputation. More than 90% of affected patients have smoked at least 20 cigarettes a day for 20 years or more.

Of the harmful substances in tobacco smoke, carbon monoxide is currently believed to be the one most heavily implicated in CV disease.

Smoking is the largest single cause of premature death in Britain. In 1985 it was shown that 22% of secondary school students regularly smoked (an *increase* of 3% on 1982). Girls aged between 14 and 15 years showed the greatest increase. Fifty-five thousand men and 22 000 women in England and Wales (1 every 7 minutes) die each year solely because they smoke. On average, about 4000 hospital beds per day are occupied as a result of smoking.

8.4 Coronary heart disease (CHD)

Otherwise known as **ischaemic heart disease**. The muscle of the heart is supplied with oxygen and nutrients by the right and left coronary arteries that flow over its surface (fig. 8.6) and whose fine branches penetrate throughout the muscle. The coronary arteries arise from two openings in the wall of the aorta just after it leaves the heart. About 5% of the blood flows through the heart muscle at rest.

Coronary, or **ischaemic heart disease** can be used as a general term for any disease which results in restriction or blockage of the coronary artery blood supply to a part of the heart. The consequence is that part of the heart will be deprived partially or completely of oxygen, a process known as **myocardial infarction** which may result in death of that part of the heart unless interconnecting blood vessels can take over the supply. Some of the detailed terminology associated with coronary heart disease can be confusing and the following summary of some of the terms used may prove useful:

> *coronary* – refers to coronary arteries.
> *thrombosis* – development of a blood clot (a *thrombus*). Associated with atheroma.
> *coronary thrombosis* – obstruction of a coronary artery or one of its branches by a blood clot. Not necessarily harmful (coronary arteries have many interconnecting branches). Sometimes simply called a *coronary*.
> *myocardial* – refers to heart muscle (*myo*–muscle, *cardial*–heart).

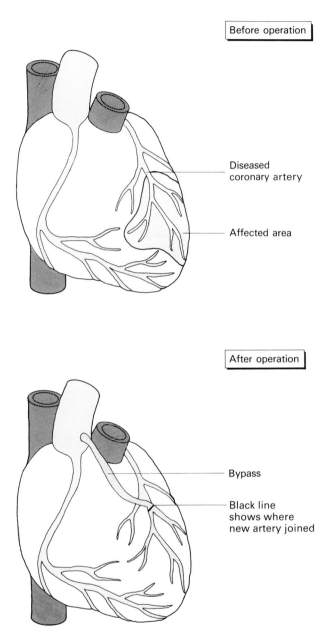

Before operation

Diseased
coronary artery

Affected area

After operation

Bypass

Black line
shows where
new artery joined

Figure 8.6 Coronary artery bypass operation, from Smith, *The Macmillan Guide to Family Health* Macmillan (1982)

infarction – suffocation due to lack of oxygen (due to narrowing or blockage of a blood vessel).

infarct – tissue damaged by infarction.

myocardial infarction – suffocation and subsequent death of heart muscle due to lack of blood (*ischaemia*). May occur by atherosclerosis (narrowing) in a coronary artery without thrombosis. The term myocardial infarction is preferred to 'coronary thrombosis' to describe a heart attack.

ischaemia – insufficient supply of blood to part of body. Myocardial ischaemia causes myocardial infarction.

ischaemic heart disease – insufficient supply of coronary blood to heart muscle. A useful general term, means the same as *coronary heart disease*.

heart attack – loose term for malfunction of the heart caused by myocardial infarction.

angina pectoris – literally 'pain in the chest'. Severe chest pain provoked by excitement/exercise/emotional stress.

Possible routes to a 'heart attack' are therefore:

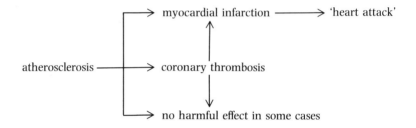

Coronary heart disease has two main forms, **angina** and **myocardial infarction** (heart attack). The **causes** of coronary heart disease are those for cardiovascular disease in general and are dealt with in section 8.8.

Angina
Signs and symptoms
Often, one of the early signs of heart disease is **angina**. The coronary arteries are relatively small and therefore easily blocked. Narrowing of the arteries by atherosclerosis reduces blood flow through them. As the situation worsens shortage of oxygen may cause angina, particularly when exercising. Cramp occurs in the heart muscle, felt as a characteristic dull **pain**, usually in the centre of the chest, which may radiate out to the neck, jaws and arms (particularly the left arm) and back. Even gentle exercise such as climbing stairs or walking across a room may bring on angina. Difficulty in breathing, sweating and dizziness may also occur. It is a common condition (roughly 0.8% of the population suffer) and does not usually require hospital treatment. As you may expect from section 8.3, it is more common among smokers and those who are overweight. It may also be caused by high blood pressure or faulty heart valves.

Treatment and prevention
Angina can severely restrict a person's activities, but symptoms can be relieved by reducing the work load on the heart, for example by stopping smoking, slimming if overweight, exercising but reducing excessive or violent exercise and avoiding stressful situations. Alternatively treatment with drugs or surgical intervention may be successful. Commonly used drugs are the **vasodilators** (e.g. nitroglycerine and amyl nitrite). They cause veins to dilate, reducing the

amount of blood returning to the heart, thereby lowering its work load. More recently a group of drugs known as **beta-blocking agents** have been introduced which block the sympathetic nervous stimulation of cells called beta-receptors in the heart and blood vessels, thus reducing heart rate to about 60 to 64 beats per minute. The reduced work rate reduces oxygen consumption of the heart by about 20%. Another group of drugs known as **calcium antagonists**, which relax arteries, may be used in conjunction with beta-blockers to improve their effectiveness.

For the 30% of patients for whom drug treatment is not effective, another alternative is a coronary artery bypass operation. This involves grafting a length of vein (from the patient's thigh) from the aorta to a point on the coronary artery beyond the original blockage, thus by-passing the blockage (see fig. 8.6). The operation has a high success rate, although it is expensive.

Coronary thrombosis and myocardial infarction (heart attack)

Coronary thrombosis is a blockage of a coronary artery by a blood clot. Starving the heart muscle of oxygen as a result of such blockage is known as **myocardial infarction** and the area affected is said to be **infarcted**. Clots tend to form at sites of atherosclerosis as described in section 8.3, so factors causing atherosclerosis are those causing coronary thrombosis. A clot that breaks off and jams further along in a narrower part is called an *embolus*. The area of heart muscle deprived of blood, and hence oxygen, will be damaged and may die, depending on the number of alternative branches along which the blood can flow through the affected area. Unfortunately, relatively few connections occur among the larger branches of the coronary arteries.

Up to 50% of patients who die of myocardial infarction reveal no coronary thrombosis at post-mortem. All, however, do show atherosclerosis. The attack may come on gradually, preceded by angina, or without warning, often when at rest. In Britain, about half a million people a year have an attack, though less than one third of them die as a result.

Signs and symptoms

The main symptom of a heart attack is a crushing central chest pain which, as with angina, may radiate out to the neck, jaws and arms. The British Heart Foundation, a heart research charity, quotes one survivor as saying 'The pain hit me like a sledgehammer. It felt as though my heart was gripped – like a vice – by a terrible, irresistible pressure'. The pain varies in degree and may be continuous or intermittent, but it does not fade away when exercise or stress ceases, unlike angina. Other symptoms are similar to those of angina (see earlier), with shortness of breath, sweating, dizziness, chills and nausea. Some of these signs and symptoms are due to physiological shock.

Severe damage to the heart has two important consequences, namely a reduced cardiac output (less blood is pumped out in a given time) and a build up of blood in the veins, increasing their blood pressure. Both of these may result in physiological shock (see below). When the heart does not pump out blood as fast as it arrives, **heart failure** is said to occur (a misleading term because the heart is still working, but not efficiently).

Infarction on the left side of the heart causes a build up of blood in the pulmonary veins. Fluid leaves the blood and enters the lungs causing difficulty in breathing and poor oxygenation of blood. Infarction on the right side causes build up of blood in the veins of the body, causing **oedema** (excess of tissue fluid) due to back pressure on the capillaries.

Signs and symptoms of reduced cardiac output are due to lack of oxygen in vital organs and include muscular weakness, fainting (mental confusion) and increased activity of the sympathetic nervous system resulting in a high heart rate (though weak pulse), cold skin and sweating. At first the sympathetic response maintains blood pressure to the brain and heart, but in the later stages of shock nerve impulses to the heart may become affected, making the situation progressively worse. Death from shock occurs in about 10% of patients who have acute myocardial infarction and may take a few hours or several days. Other signs and symptoms of shock include low body temperature, and kidney failure due to low blood pressure.

Treatment and prevention
Following a heart attack, or even if early symptoms are thought to be developing, a doctor or an ambulance should be called immediately, and the patient kept warm and allowed to rest comfortably. If the patient becomes unconscious, appropriate first aid should be administered, which will include cardiac massage if the heart has stopped beating and mouth-to-mouth resuscitation if breathing has stopped. It is easy to learn to administer aid such as this and it is increasingly being recognised that, even if no other first aid is learned, as many people as possible should be acquainted with these basic techniques. The British Red Cross and St John's Ambulance Brigade organise training sessions. Resuscitation by medical staff may involve electrical stimulation of the heart or injection of a heart stimulant such as digitalis.

The serious complications usually occur within a few hours and this is when most deaths occur. The patient may be allowed to recuperate at home or be transferred to a special coronary unit or intensive care unit in a hospital. While in intensive care, the patient is permanently connected to an electrocardiograph (ECG) which monitors electrical activity of the heart and shows up any irregularities of rhythm. Blood pressure, temperature, pulse rate, fluid intake and urine output are monitored (why?) and blood samples taken, particularly for presence of enzymes associated with damage to heart muscle, such as creatine phosphokinase (CPK) and glutamic oxaloacetic transaminase (SGOT).

Pain relief by drugs may be given, as well as oxygen by means of a mask to reduce the work load on the heart. For the first two days at least, the patient is usually confined to bed, but gentle exercise is encouraged as soon as possible to start exercising the heart muscle again. A light, low-salt diet is usual at first. Anticoagulant drugs may be taken orally to reduce the risk of blood clots developing in veins. Diuretic drugs are used to stimulate kidney activity. This in turn relieves blood pressure, reducing breathlessness and swelling of the ankles and legs. Beta-blockers (see Treatment and Prevention of Angina) lower the rates of post-heart attack deaths.

If irregularities of the heart persist, an intravenous drip may be used. This consists of a small needle placed in a vein and connected to a bottle containing glucose solution and a suitable drug. Alternatively, electrical stimulation of the heart may be required. In an emergency, a cardiac defibrillator, which administers a short, sharp electric shock is used. Alternatively if the normal electrical pacemaking of the heart is temporarily damaged, an artificial electrical pacemaker may be used for a few days.

The patient is usually kept in hospital for between 10 days and 3 weeks. Return to work within a further few weeks is possible and complete recovery can be made in some cases. However, a change in lifestyle may be recommended to reduce the likelihood of further attacks (see Risk Factors below). Despite controversy as to the role of certain factors such as diet in predisposing to further heart attacks, there is common agreement that smoking and overeating should be avoided, and that regular exercise is beneficial.

Are you at risk?
An attempt to produce a rough guide to the risk factors involved in heart disease has been made by the Michigan Heart Association and is presented in table 8.1. Risk factors (not in order of importance) include: maleness, age, heredity, high blood pressure (more than 160/95), obesity, diabetes, behaviour (aggressive, competitive, urgent personalities).

Avoidable risk factors include:
1 excess saturated fat and cholesterol in diet
2 cigarette smoking
3 lack of physical exercise
4 possibly emotional stress
5 possibly soft drinking water

Combinations of risk factors greatly increase the likelihood of heart disease. For example, *taking the 3 major risk factors*, smoking, high blood pressure and high blood cholesterol, the death rate for men aged 30–59 years is:

no risk factor	1 in 50
one risk factor	1 in 20 (risk doubled)
two risk factors	1 in 11 (risk quadrupled)
all three risk factors	1 in 6 (risk 8 times as great).

To avoid heart disease the 3 most positive steps that one can take are:
1 don't smoke
2 eat a well-planned diet – do not become overweight
3 make aerobic exercise a regular part of your lifestyle

8.5 Strokes – cerebral thrombosis and cerebral haemorrhage

A stroke, or **cerebro-vascular accident** as it is medically known, is sudden interference with the circulation of arterial blood to a part of the brain, usually resulting in some permanent damage due to lack of oxygen.

About 10% of deaths in the U.K. are caused by strokes. In an average year 1 person in 500 in Britain will have a stroke. About 1 in 2 to 1 in 3 is fatal within a month, and about 1 in 3 causes permanent disability. It is second only to heart disease as a cause of premature death in Britain. In most countries the incidence is falling in both sexes.

Table 8.1 Risk chart for heart disease. Devised by the Michigan Heart Association and published in *The Sunday Times New Book of Body Maintenance* Mermaid Books, Ed. Gillie, O. et al. (1982).

Sex	Blood pressure	Fat % in diet	Exercise	Tobacco smoking	Weight	Heredity	Age
Female under 40 1	100 (upper reading) 1	Diet contains no animal or solid fats 1	Intensive work and recreational exertion 2	Non-user 0	More than 5lb. below standard weight 0	No known history of heart disease 1	10 to 20 1
Female 40–50 2	120 (upper reading) 2	Diet contains soft margarine, no fried food 2	Moderate work and recreational exertion 2	Cigar and/or pipe 1	−5 to +5lb. standard weight 1	1 relative over 60 with cardiovascular disease 2	21 to 30 2
Female over 50 3	140 (upper reading) 3	Diet contains some butter or hard margarine, some fried food 3	Sedentary work and intense recreational exertion 3	10 cigarettes or less a day 2	6–20lb. overweight 2	2 relatives over 60 with cardiovascular disease 3	31 to 40 3
Male 5	160 (upper reading) 4	Diet contains a lot of butter, or hard margarine, or fried food 4	Sedentary work and moderate recreational exertion 5	20 cigarettes a day 4	21–35lb. overweight 3	1 relative under 60 with cardiovascular disease 4	41 to 50 4

Stocky male 6	180 (upper reading) 6	Daily diet contains butter, or hard margarine or fried food 5	Sedentary work and light recreational exertion 6	30 cigarettes a day 6	36–50lb. overweight 5	2 relatives under 60 with cardiovascular disease 6	51 to 60 5
Bald stocky male 7	200 or over (upper reading) 8	Daily diet contains butter, or hard margarine, and fried food 7	Complete lack of all exercise 8	40 cigarettes a day or more 10	51–65lb. overweight 7	3 relatives under 60 with cardiovascular disease 7	61 to 70 and over 8

1. If you are a smoker who inhales deeply and smokes to a short butt, add 1 to your total.
2. If you have passed an insurance company medical recently, your blood pressure will probably be below 140.
3. Don't forget that cream, butter and eggs are high in animal fat.
4. To calculate the hereditary factor, only count parents, grandparents, brothers and sisters as relatives.

If you are an aggressive person, live under a lot of stress or suffer from gout or diabetes, then these factors will increase the risk of heart disease. But they are too complicated to calculate on a points system.

Scores:

6 to 11 – well below average risk
12 to 17 – below average risk
18 to 24 – average risk
25 to 31 – moderate risk
32 to 40 – dangerous risk
41 to 63 – imminent danger: see your doctor

Causes

There are 2 main types of stroke, namely **cerebral thrombosis** and **cerebral haemorrhage**. Both types are usually the result of atherosclerosis, which has been described in section 8.3, and therefore have similar causes. About a quarter of strokes are caused by cerebral thrombosis where a blood clot cuts off blood supply to part of the brain. Typically the blood clot develops on an atherosclerotic deposit in a major cerebral artery. About three quarters of strokes are caused by rupture (haemorrhage) of a cerebral artery, described as **cerebral haemorrhage**. This may be caused by excess blood pressure (hypertension) or may occur because the artery has been weakened by atherosclerosis.

The main risk factors for strokes are thus atherosclerosis and high blood pressure. There is less association with high cholesterol levels than with coronary heart disease but a greater link with obesity. Smoking is also regarded as a high risk factor.

Signs and symptoms

The effects of a stroke depend entirely on how much of the brain has been damaged. The extremes are for there to be no effect or for the damage to be fatal. In between, more or less any degree of impairment is possible. Figure 8.7 shows the two cerebral hemispheres, in which conscious thought is located. The right hemisphere controls the left side of the body and the left the right. With strokes, the middle cerebral artery, which supplies the motor cortex (fig. 8.7) is frequently affected on one side of the brain. As a result, the opposite side of the body becomes completely or partially paralysed. If the sensory cortex is damaged there will be loss of sensation from the opposite half of the body. A limb, or a hand for example, may seem not to belong to the affected person. In trying to rationalise the experience, it has been known for patients to object to sharing the bed with another person, to accuse doctors of playing tricks by attaching somebody else's limb to them, or, for example, for only one of a pair of gloves to be put on because there is no felt image of the other hand in the brain.

Branches of the middle cerebral artery supply the language centres in the left temporal lobe. Damage here can cause a variety of language problems such as inability to understand incoming sounds. Even if the language is still understood, it may be impossible to speak coherently, an extremely frustrating experience. Blockage of the posterior cerebral artery causes partial or complete blindness. Personality changes could follow if the anterior cerebral artery is affected. Confusion and loss of memory are further common symptoms.

Recently it has been realised that old people often have minor strokes (**transient ischaemic attacks**) which are barely noticeable. Signs or symptoms typical of a stroke appear in mild form for a few minutes followed by total recovery. These may include sudden violent headache; blurred or double vision; temporary deafness or ringing in the ears; weakness; numbness in arms, legs or face (usually on one side of the body); temporary memory loss; personality change; inability to walk; slight droop at the corner of the mouth.

Treatment

The brain has great powers of recovery given the right exercise, encouragement and drug treatment. Speech therapists and physiotherapists have key

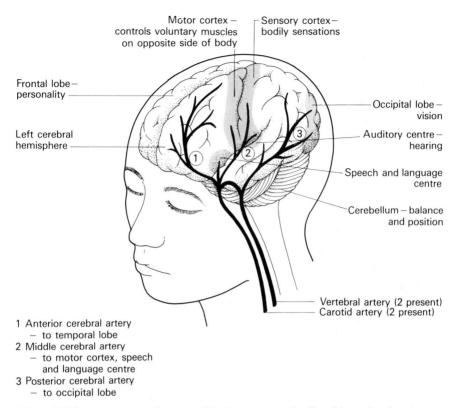

Motor cortex –
controls voluntary muscles
on opposite side of body

Sensory cortex –
bodily sensations

Frontal lobe –
personality

Left cerebral
hemisphere

Occipital lobe –
vision

Auditory centre –
hearing

Speech and language
centre

Cerebellum – balance
and position

Vertebral artery (2 present)
Carotid artery (2 present)

1 Anterior cerebral artery
 – to temporal lobe
2 Middle cerebral artery
 – to motor cortex, speech
 and language centre
3 Posterior cerebral artery
 – to occipital lobe

Figure 8.7 The main areas and arteries of the brain commonly affected by strokes, based on a diagram from Smith, *The Macmillan Guide to Family Health* Macmillan (1982)

roles. Doctors and occupational therapists may also be involved. The speech therapist can help a person to talk intelligibly again. A physiotherapist will help the victim to exercise the appropriate muscles, either so that other muscles can take over from paralysed muscle, or to help regain use of the latter.

Actions such as walking and feeding may have to be relearned by the patient and this may take as long as it would take a child having to learn things for the first time. Parts of the brain next to the damaged areas may have to take over the role of the damaged areas. Constant reassurance and encouragement are required because recovery is slow and it is very easy for the patient to become depressed or frustrated and to give up. Only determined effort is likely to succeed.

Rehabilitation should be started as soon as possible after the stroke. Anti-coagulant drugs may be given to prevent blood clotting if this has been the cause. Drugs to lower blood pressure may be given. Smoking is discouraged. Understanding of the condition is important for everyone associated with the victim. If, for example, the victim speaks nonsense, the listener may believe the victim is 'mentally deficient', when in fact the victim may be able to hear and reason perfectly well but simply be unable to 'make the right words come out'. The victim is a prisoner in his or her own body. Communication can be established by devices like 'squeeze my hand for yes', 'blink twice for no'.

It should also be remembered that a stroke victim suffers the extra burden of having suffered a *sudden* change in circumstances, perhaps from being an apparently healthy, active individual to being confined to a hospital bed or wheelchair, with constant nursing. Extra physical, emotional and financial strain may be imposed on an elderly partner or other close relative, and if the victim is to live at home, suitable adaptations in the home environment may be needed to cope with particular handicaps like paralysis. The home help service provided by Social Services is available as a back-up for help at home. Home or community nurses are also provided by every District Health Authority to give nursing care for patients at home.

Support for stroke victims and their close relatives and friends comes from the Chest, Heart and Stroke Association who can give the addresses of the nearest local self-help groups.

8.6   Social implications of cardiovascular disease

The social implications of cardiovascular disease are many and profound. Many will be clear from the discussion so far in chapter 8, but the following is a summary of some of the important implications which could be discussed further.

1   Cost to Health Service
2   In connection with improved preventive measures or treatment:
    – prolonging of life
    – improved quality of life for individuals
    – advantages to family of parent surviving
3   Heart transplants
    – improving technology
    – donor cards
4   Diet:
    – counselling services and education
    – change
    – food labelling
    – advertising. The food industry currently spends £135 million per year on advertising. Should more be spent on advertising *healthy* foods? Should there be Government intervention to enforce this?
    – education
5   Smoking:
    – counselling services and education
    – non-smoking areas in public places
    – sports and arts sponsorship by tobacco companies
    – advertising restrictions/bans
    – risk categories. Smoking is strongly correlated with social class. In 1984, 17% of professional men and 15% of professional women smoked compared with 49% of unskilled men and 36% of unskilled women. Of men in work, 36% smoke; 61% of unemployed men smoke.
6   Exercise:
    – education and attitudes, particularly among children; emphasis on positive benefits of exercise
    – provision of facilities

9 Physical fitness

9.1 The concept of physical fitness

Most of us will have our own preconceived ideas about what is meant by physical fitness. Here are some definitions taken from various sources.

Physical fitness is:

'. . . a person's ability to utilise the machinery of their body in sports and exercise.'

'. . . the ability of your whole body, including the muscles, skeleton, heart and all other body parts, to work together efficiently, which means being able to do the most work with the least amount of effort.'

'. . . the ability to carry out daily tasks with vigour and alertness, without undue fatigue, and with ample energy remaining to enjoy leisure-time pursuits and to meet unusual situations and unforeseen emergencies.'

'. . . the capacity to meet successfully the present and potential physical challenges of life.'

From a biologist's point of view, the reference to machinery in the first definition is useful. Just as we need to be aware of how a machine works in order to keep it running smoothly and efficiently, so we need to be aware of the needs of our own bodies. The important difference between a non-living and a *living* machine is that the latter is self-renewing and responds to use by maintaining or even improving itself. In other words, it becomes physically fit. Conversely, if it is not used, or if it is abused, it will decline in performance, that is, become unfit.

In recent years there has been a growing awareness of the benefits of maintaining a physically fit body. Some of these are listed below:

- improved health, e.g. reduced risk of cardiovascular disease, improved resistance to infection, improved respiratory fitness
- remedial – can help remedy asthma, obesity, poor posture (less likelihood of back pain), injuries
- improved co-ordination, mental alertness
- relaxation because it reduces stress
- preparation for leisure; social benefits
- personal expression – dance, gymnastics
- improved quality of life – look good, feel good
- increased longevity
- enjoyment of a physical challenge
- enjoyment of competition
- possibly preparation for a career

A more scientific analysis of the benefits of physical fitness identifies eleven parts to physical fitness, five being **health-related** and six **skill-related**:

Health-related fitness
1 **cardiovascular and respiratory fitness** – heart, lungs and circulation
2 **strength** – muscular force
3 **endurance** – using the muscles over extended time periods
4 **flexibility** – using the joints
5 **body composition** – body fatness

Skill-related fitness
1 **agility** – changing position quickly
2 **balance**
3 **coordination**
4 **power** – strength and speed
5 **reaction time**
6 **speed**

Table 9.1 summarises the health-related benefits of certain sports and other activities. In sections 9.2, 9.3 and 9.4 a detailed examination of the body's response to exercise should lead to a better understanding of the concept of physical fitness. At this early point it is important to distinguish between aerobic and anaerobic exercise. **Aerobic exercise** promotes the body's ability to use oxygen efficiently. Aerobic activities, or 'aerobics', include dance, certain exercise routines, jogging, marathon running and swimming. They are associated with development of a healthy cardiovascular and respiratory system, as well as muscular endurance. Medical experts agreed at an international conference in 1982 that aerobic fitness is the type that correlates best with health. Aerobic exercises are typically longer lasting and gentler than those required to develop anaerobic fitness. **Anaerobic exercise**, such as weightlifting, shotputting and sprinting, uses power and is explosive. The energy is supplied mainly by anaerobic respiration and so the heart and lungs do not receive much stimulation.

With the increased awareness of the benefits of physical fitness, there has been a movement towards broadening of the range of physical activities undertaken both within schools and colleges, and by the adult population. Non-competitive activities like jogging and aerobics have surged in popularity. What is the origin of this movement? It comes from an awareness that some of the most important diseases of western society are related not to infection and poor standards of hygiene, as in the past, but to poor understanding of our own bodies as machines and how to maintain a healthy body. In the years since the Second World War a dramatic rise has been noted in certain, largely avoidable, diseases and problems such as heart disease, atherosclerosis, obesity, hypertension, back pain, and lung cancer, as already described in chapters 7 and 8. As the causes of these diseases and problems became more clearly understood, the importance of diet and physical fitness emerged very strongly.

Health problems relating to, or caused by, lack of exercise are described as **hypokinetic conditions**. Hypokinetic diseases are still rising in incidence. It is becoming clear that the problems often begin early in childhood, where there is concern on two fronts. Firstly, too much time is spent in passive pursuits such as watching television or riding in cars rather than cycling or walking. Recent data suggest that children are often **not** as active as they often appear and that activity seldom reaches a level sufficient to promote cardiovascular health. Secondly, poor diet and smoking are common among children and the beginnings of atherosclerosis can be detected in childhood. One third of all American teenagers have been shown to have weight problems. Thus keeping fit has now

Table 9.1 Health-related benefits of sports and other activities (Baxdon *Fitness for Life*, Teacher's Edition, 2nd ed., Corbin, C.B. & Lindsey, R., Scott Foresman & Co. (1983)).

Sport or Activity	Develops Cardiovascular Fitness	Develops Strength	Develops Muscular Endurance	Develops Flexibility	Helps Control Fatness
Archery	Poor	Fair	Poor	Poor	Poor
Backpacking, Hiking	Good	Good	Excellent	Fair	Good
Badminton	Good	Poor	Fair	Fair	Good
Basketball	Excellent	Poor	Fair	Poor	Good
Canoeing	Fair	Poor	Fair	Poor	Fair
Dance, Ballet	Good	Good	Good	Excellent	Fair
Dance, Disco	Good	Poor	Good	Fair	Good
Dance, Modern	Good	Fair	Good	Excellent	Good
Fencing	Fair	Fair	Good	Fair	Fair
Field Hockey	Excellent	Fair	Good	Fair	Good
Golf (walking)	Fair	Poor	Poor	Fair	Fair
Gymnastics	Fair	Excellent	Excellent	Excellent	Fair
Horseback Riding	Poor	Poor	Poor	Poor	Poor
Judo, Karate	Poor	Fair	Fair	Fair	Poor
Mountain Climbing	Good	Good	Good	Poor	Fair
Rowing, Crew	Excellent	Fair	Excellent	Poor	Excellent
Sailing	Poor	Poor	Poor	Poor	Poor
Skating, Ice	Good	Poor	Good	Poor	Fair
Skating, Roller	Fair	Poor	Fair	Poor	Fair
Skiing, Cross-Country	Excellent	Fair	Good	Poor	Excellent
Skiing, Downhill	Poor	Fair	Fair	Poor	Poor
Snooker; Billiards	Poor	Poor	Poor	Poor	Poor
Soccer	Excellent	Fair	Good	Fair	Good
Squash	Fair	Poor	Fair	Fair	Fair
Table Tennis	Poor*	Poor	Poor	Poor	Poor
Tennis	Fair	Poor	Fair	Poor	Fair

come to be regarded as just one aspect of what should be a healthy life style. Other important aspects include diet, smoking habits and use of drugs such as alcohol.

Physical fitness is therefore now regarded as an important paediatric problem (one concerning children), involving not only children but parents, teachers and the whole community.

Active intervention programmes involving education can be very effective. In 1968, for example, the chance of an American middle-aged man dying from ischaemic heart disease was 40% greater than that of an Englishman, but 10 years later, after the Americans had devoted huge resources to combating the problem, the chances were lower than for an Englishman and the number of deaths was decreasing. Despite this, Dr Kenneth Cooper, founder of the Institute for Aerobics Research in the U.S.A., which conducted national tests on over 2 million schoolchildren in the schoolyear 1985–1986, reports that youth fitness levels in the U.S.A. are alarmingly low. Apparently the fitness craze which has swept the adult population has not yet reached America's youth. Dr Cooper says, 'We have made giant strides in reducing death by heart disease in the U.S. through fitness programmes for adults, but we will never be successful until we make the young realise that what they do with their bodies *now* will determine how those bodies will carry them through their lives – and for how long'. Details of this survey are available from P.E.A. (see p. 123). According to another source, 40% of all children aged 5 to 8 years show at least one of the following three heart disease risk factors: high blood pressure, high blood cholesterol, physical inactivity. Evidence that physical fitness can reduce heart disease has come from a number of scientific enquiries. An often quoted discovery, made in 1953, is of the higher incidence of heart disease in London bus drivers than conductors on double deck buses. The latter were more active as a result of walking and climbing stairs as part of their job. Further studies have shown that physical activity at work is correlated with a reduced incidence of coronary heart disease.

Hopefully, **'health-related fitness'** programmes in schools from an early age can help to promote the necessary changes in lifestyle. Cooperation between different subjects like biology and P.E. can add a new dimension to education and stimulate interest. Emphasis needs to be placed on activities that can be followed into adult life, on enjoying physical exercise and the benefits it can bring, and on understanding *why* exercise is beneficial. In addition, individual fitness programmes can be designed so that people learn how to monitor their own fitness, (see section 9.5).

9.2   Effects of exercise on muscles

Practically every movement of the body is brought about by the contraction and relaxation of muscles. Even when the body is supposedly at rest, muscle 'tone' is being preserved whereby posture and readiness for action are maintained by partial contraction of muscles. Muscles also help to protect and keep body organs in position.

Some muscles are under voluntary control (the skeletal or voluntary muscles); others, such as those in the bladder, intestines and walls of blood vessels, are involuntary and perform their functions without control from the will. The heart is a special muscle and will be considered further in section 9.4. There are over 500 voluntary muscles in the body and they make up roughly 40% of our body weight.

In order to understand the effects of exercise on muscles, some knowledge of the physiology of muscle contraction and the concept of oxygen debt is helpful, and this can be obtained from standard 'A' level biology textbooks.

Long-term effects of exercise on muscles and muscle performance

1   *Muscle size*
    Basic muscle size is genetically determined, i.e. inherited from one's parents. The level of testosterone secreted affects the development of the muscles, and the higher levels of testosterone in males are largely responsible for men having larger muscles than women. However,

exercise can increase the size of muscles by up to 60%, notably specific strength training tasks. This is mainly due to an increase in the diameter of individual muscle fibres, but an increase in numbers of fibres also occurs. Within the fibres, there is an increase in the number of myofibrils.

2 *Biochemical changes*

Within the fibres the number and size of mitochondria increase in response to exercise. Those biochemical processes that take place in mitochondria such as Krebs cycle, electron transport and oxidation of fatty acids, all occur more rapidly in the muscle as a result. After *endurance* (rather than strength) training, the ability of mitochondria to generate ATP can be doubled. More creatine phosphate is stored, and up to twice as much glycogen and fat are stored. More myoglobin (a haemoglobin-like molecule that stores oxygen in muscles) is present and hence more oxygen is stored. The effect of these changes is less reliance on anaerobic respiration and therefore less lactic acid is produced. There is greater ability to release fatty acids from fat stores and so use them for energy. Fit people therefore use more fat during exercise than unfit people.

3 *Increase in muscle strength, power and endurance*

Muscle strength, power and endurance can all be increased by exercise. **Strength** is mainly determined by size and represents the *maximum* force that can be exerted by a muscle at a given moment in time.

Power is the amount of work that can be done in a given period of time, and depends on both strength and speed of contraction of the muscle. The initial power that can be provided rapidly diminishes. **Endurance** is related to the efficiency of supplying fuel to keep the muscle working over long periods. It is related to exercise and to other factors, particularly diet. A person on a high carbohydrate diet would have a larger store of glycogen in the body and thus have greater endurance.

Exercise increases the *strength* of a muscle only if the muscle is working against a load (resistance) greater than that to which it is normally accustomed. Either intensity or duration of exercise can be increased to achieve this. Muscles working at, or near, their maximum force of contraction increase strength very rapidly, even if the exercise period is confined to several minutes only a day. Optimal increase in muscle strength can be achieved by 6 maximal/near maximal muscle contractions performed on 3 separate occasions daily for 3 days per week. An increase in strength of about 30%, taking 6 to 8 weeks, is usually achieved in the untrained person. This corresponds to a 30% increase in size of the exercised muscle.

Three types of strength have been recognised, namely **static, explosive** and **dynamic**. Static strength is a measure of the force that can be applied to an immovable object, as in a tug of war. Explosive strength, required for example in jumping and throwing, is a measure of the force that can be exerted in one explosive act. Dynamic strength is used in working over an extended time period, e.g. in running or rowing. Each type of strength can be increased with relevant exercises.

It is important to realise that just to *maintain* strength of muscle, exercise is needed. When muscles are *not* exercised regularly they quickly revert to their former state and get 'out of condition', losing both speed of contraction and strength. They lose their ability to use oxygen efficiently and aerobic fitness declines faster than anaerobic fitness. Lactic acid is more likely to be produced and this in turn decreases endurance.

4 *Blood supply to muscles*
Regular exercise results in an increase in the number of blood vessels supplying blood to the muscles, thus providing a more efficient transport system for oxygen, glucose and removal of waste.

5 *Coordination*
Exercise improves the coordination between muscles, particularly between pairs of antagonistic muscles (muscles which work in opposition to each other to achieve movement of a particular joint). More skilful movement is therefore possible.

Exercise also improves the speed at which muscles relax as well as contract. When one of a pair of antagonistic muscles contracts, the other relaxes. If it does not relax rapidly enough, it may be torn by the pulling effect of the other muscle.

Short-term effects of exercise on muscles

1 *Blood flow*
The blood supply to muscles may increase by up to 25 times during exercise as a result of effects on the gas exchange and cardiovascular systems (see sections 9.3 and 9.4).

2 *Respiration and oxygen debt*
During the first few seconds of light exercise and during the whole of short duration heavy exercise (up to 2 minutes), ATP is mainly produced as a result of anaerobic respiration. As a result of anaerobic respiration an oxygen debt may build up. Maximum oxygen debt is about 10 to 12 litres (up to 18 litres in a trained athlete).

3 *Fatigue and exhaustion*
As a result of exercise muscular fatigue may occur. This is the inability to repeat muscular contractions with the same force. Exhaustion is reached when further contraction becomes extremely difficult or impossible.

4 *Damage to muscle fibres*
Excessively hard training can damage muscle fibres, for example by tearing or straining tissue through over-stretching. Warming-up exercises can help to reduce the likelihood of this. After relatively heavy exercise muscles tend to become shorter and tighter and thus more prone to injury. Flexibility exercises can help to overcome this by gently stretching muscles. Muscle soreness is a normal response to unusually high demands on a muscle. The exact cause is unknown. It

is probably due to swelling during recovery, and repair of minor damage, and can be relieved by gentle exercise.

5 *Cramp*

Cramp is the sudden powerful contraction of muscle tissue which can result from over-exercise. Any activity which results in lactic acid build up (lack of oxygen) increases the risk of cramp. Chilling and lack of salt increase the risk.

6 *Depletion of glycogen and potassium*

Stores of glycogen and potassium can be depleted after hard exercise. These may take several days to build up again.

9.3 Effects of exercise on gas exchange

During exercise, there is a greater demand for oxygen by the muscles for oxidation of glucose and fatty acids in aerobic respiration. At the same time more carbon dioxide will be produced. The ability to increase rate of gas exchange at the muscles is therefore important, and may be the limiting factor in determining the amount of work that the muscles can perform. Anaerobic exercise, such as weightlifting and short sprints, is not so dependent on gas exchange because oxygen is not needed. Aerobic endurance tasks, however, such as long-distance running or jogging, are heavily dependent on the body making adjustments to gas exchange. The effect of exercise on gas exchange between the lungs and the atmosphere will be examined later in this section. The effect on the cardiovascular system, which has the role of transporting respiratory gases between the lungs and the body tissues, is dealt with in section 9.4. It will be seen that it is the cardiovascular system that is the limiting factor in supplying oxygen to the muscles, not gas exchange in the lungs.

Changes in ventilation (breathing)

Ventilation can be measured in the laboratory using a spirometer (see standard 'A' level biology texts) as mentioned in section 9.5. Figure 9.1 shows some of the lung volumes and capacities that can be measured with a spirometer and a typical trace before and after exercise.

As a result of exercise, total gas exchanged in a given time period (**pulmonary ventilation**) is increased in two ways. Firstly, *depth* of breathing (**tidal volume**) can increase, and secondly *rate* of breathing (**ventilation rate**). Both of these can be seen to have occurred in fig. 9.1(b).

Pulmonary ventilation (PV) = ventilation rate × tidal volume

It has been shown that initially there is a linear relationship between pulmonary ventilation and oxygen consumption, that is an increase in total ventilation results in a corresponding increase in oxygen consumption. About 25 litres of pulmonary ventilation are required per litre of oxygen used. At high pulmonary ventilations, however (more than 80 litres per minute), pulmonary ventilation increases more rapidly than oxygen consumption, showing that inefficiencies are beginning to occur. Some typical figures for a young adult male are given below. Figures for females are typically about 80% of those for males.

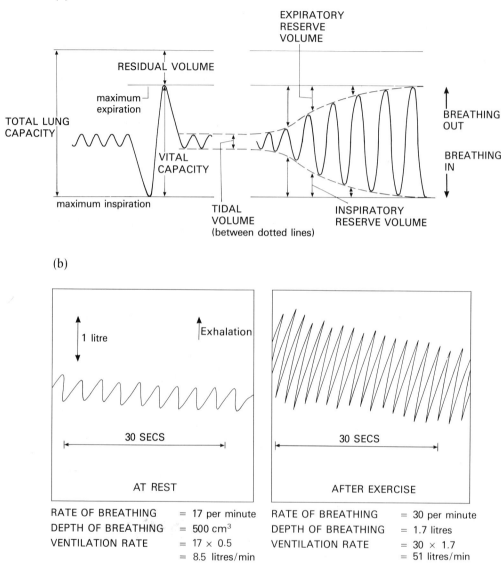

Figure 9.1 (a) Lung volumes and lung capacities. Note: the Figure shows a spirometer trace. As the subject breathes out, the lid fills and the lid and pen rise; as the subject breathes in, the lid empties and the lid and pen fall. Published spirometer traces are often *inverted* to show the line rising as the subject breathes in and descending as the subject breathes out.
(b) Spirometer trace before and after exercise. Definitions: *Tidal volume:* volume of gas exchanged during one breath in and out. *Vital capacity:* maximum volume of air that can be exchanged during one breath in and out. *Residual volume:* volume of air (about 1.5 litres) remaining in the lungs even after forced expiration. It cannot be expelled. *Inspiratory reserve volume:* volume of extra air that could be inhaled after normal inspiration. *Expiratory reserve volume:* volume of extra air that could be forced out after normal expiration

114

Tidal volume at rest: 0.45 litres
Tidal volume after maximal exercise: 3 litres
Ventilation rate at rest: 15 breaths per minute (10 to 20)
Ventilation rate after maximal exercise: 40 to 45 breaths per minute
Pulmonary ventilation at rest: 6.75 litres per minute
Pulmonary ventilation after exercise: 100 to 110 litres per minute
Maximum breathing capacity: 150 to 170 litres per minute
Oxygen consumption at rest: 0.25 to 0.4 litres per minute
Oxygen consumption after maximal exercise: 3.6 litres per minute (up to 5.1 litres per minute for marathon runners)
Vital capacity 5.7 litres male; 4.25 litres female

The maximum possible increase in pulmonary ventilation and oxygen consumption between rest and maximal exercise is about a 20-fold increase. The relative importance of changes in *depth* of breathing and *rate* of breathing can be investigated using the spirometer and interesting comparisons made between, for example, smokers and non-smokers or 'fit' and 'unfit' people. It is important when making comparisons though to ensure a standard amount of exercise is done, for example by using a bicycle ergometer (see section 9.5).

At rest, expiration takes longer than inspiration. This is because expiration is mainly a passive process, relying on elastic recoil of lung tissue and dropping of the rib cage under gravity. After exercise, however, the internal intercostal muscles contract much more strongly to achieve a forced expiration of air by moving the ribs vigorously downwards. The abdominal muscles also contract strongly, causing more rapid *upward* movement of the diaphragm. The increase in tidal volume in response to exercise is brought about through the use of both inspiratory reserve volume and expiratory reserve volume; in other words, a person inspires more deeply *and* expires more forcefully. The tidal volume even at maximal exercise rarely exceeds 50% of the vital capacity; in other words, only half the possible depth of breathing is used.

Changes in diffusion rate of oxygen and carbon dioxide and flow of blood through lung capillaries

The **oxygen diffusing capacity**, the rate at which oxygen can diffuse from the alveoli into the blood, increases during exercise. During maximal exercise, it can as much as treble. The improvement is due mainly to a greater rate of blood flow through the capillaries around the alveoli, in turn due to higher cardiac output (see section 9.4). Also in response to exercise, the sympathetic nervous system and secretion of adrenaline are stimulated. These act on smooth muscle in the capillaries, bringing about vasodilation, and hence a larger volume of blood (see also section 9.4). A better supply of oxygen and nutrients, and more efficient removal of waste products is thus ensured. The **diffusing capacity of carbon dioxide** also increases during exercise, but this is of no significance because carbon dioxide can diffuse 20 times more rapidly than oxygen and this would be fast enough even if its diffusing capacity were unaltered. The sympathetic nervous system and secretion of adrenaline also stimulate the smooth muscle in the bronchioles, making it relax, causing dilation (expansion) of the bronchioles. Resistance to passage of air is thus reduced to about half.

Regulation of breathing

The control of breathing by the central nervous system is outside the scope of this book, but it should be remembered that the most important factor bringing about a rise in pulmonary ventilation during exercise is thought to be the rise in carbon dioxide levels in the arterial blood. Lowering of oxygen also has an effect. Chemoreceptors in the carotid and aortic bodies are involved, as well as the respiratory centre in the medulla of the brain.

Dissociation of oxygen from haemoglobin

Unloading (**dissociation**) of oxygen from haemoglobin is stimulated by relatively low partial pressures (concentrations) of oxygen in the tissues. The more vigorous the exercise, the greater is the reduction in oxygen levels in the muscles and the faster and more efficient is the release of oxygen from the haemoglobin. The simultaneous rise in the partial pressure of carbon dioxide during exercise further increases the unloading of oxygen from haemoglobin (the Bohr effect).

The body responds extremely rapidly to the demands of exercise and the gas exchange system is so efficient that virtually no change in the oxygen level of *arterial* blood leaving the heart, and only a minor increase in carbon dioxide level of the same *arterial* blood can be detected during exercise, although notable differences do occur in the veins.

9.4   Effects of exercise on the cardiovascular system

The cardiovascular system (CV system), namely the heart and blood vessels of the body, has already been studied in chapter 8 in relation to disease. Cardiovascular disease is a major killer and hence it is not surprising that the effect of exercise on the CV system, particularly on the fitness of the system, is a subject of much current interest.

Our concern in this section is to examine the role of the CV system in supplying oxygen and nutrients to, and removing carbon dioxide and heat from, the tissues of the body, particularly muscles, because it is this function which is most directly relevant to exercise. As already noted earlier, the oxygen demand in muscles after exercise can increase by as much as 20-fold. It is believed by many physiologists that the efficiency of the CV system in supplying oxygen is the major limiting factor in the amount of work the muscles can perform.

A discussion of factors controlling the heart beat (nervous system, chemicals, self-regulation) will be found in standard A-level biology textbooks.

Cardiac output, heart rate and stroke volume

Cardiac output is the amount of blood pumped out by the heart in a given time. Some typical figures are given below:

> At rest: 4 to 6 litres per minute
> After maximal exercise: young adult male 22 litres per minute (30 $l\,min^{-1}$ for an athlete)
> young adult female 15 litres per minute

The effect of maximal exercise is thus to increase the cardiac output about 4-

fold. The lungs, which receive blood direct from the heart, therefore receive 4 times the usual amount of blood. The response is very rapid, as personal experience of a faster, stronger pulse in response to exercise will confirm. Cardiac output is a product of two variables, **heart rate** (the number of beats per minute) and **stroke volume** (the amount of blood pumped out of the heart at each beat).

Cardiac output = heart rate × stroke volume

Heart rate is easily measured as the pulse rate, but stroke volume can only be measured by elaborate techniques. Roughly speaking, heart rate can triple and stroke volume double in response to maximal exercise. Some typical figures for heart rate and stroke volume are given below. Note that a cardiac output of 30 litres per minute means **both** ventricles are pumping out 30 litres per minute. This would fill a bath (26 gallons) in two minutes.

At rest – untrained	*At rest* – trained
Heart rate = 65 to 70 beats per min (50 to 75 normal)	Heart rate = 50 beats per min
Stroke vol = 77 cm³	Stroke vol = 105 cm³
Cardiac output = 5 litres per min	Cardiac output = 5.25 litres per min
After maximal exercise – untrained	*After maximal exercise* – trained
Heart rate = 195	Heart rate = 185
Stroke vol = 110 cm³	Stroke vol = 162 cm³
Cardiac output = 21.5 litres per min	Cardiac output = 30 litres per min

Effect of training on cardiac output

It has already been shown that muscles increase in size in response to training, and the heart is no exception. Increases in size (muscle mass and size of chambers) of about 40% can occur as a result of aerobic endurance training, such as a marathon runner would undertake. A 40% greater cardiac output is thus achieved. Anaerobic exercise, such as sprint training, does little to increase size of heart muscle.

At rest the cardiac output of an athlete is much the same as an average person, but because the heart is stronger this would be achieved by a stronger beat (larger stroke volume) at a lower number of beats per minute. Figure 9.2 shows how an increase in cardiac output from 5 to 30 litres per minute is achieved in a marathon runner. Note that maximum stroke volume is achieved at about half the required cardiac output and that further increase in cardiac output is achieved solely by an increase in heart rate.

Blood pressure

Increased cardiac output raises blood pressure in the arteries during exercise, usually by about 30%. In addition, in order to divert blood to muscles, heart and lungs, vasoconstriction (narrowing) of arterioles occurs in those tissues and organs which are in less immediate need of oxygen, mainly the gut, liver, kidneys and spleen, and vasodilation (opening) of arterioles occurs in muscles (see below), heart and lungs.

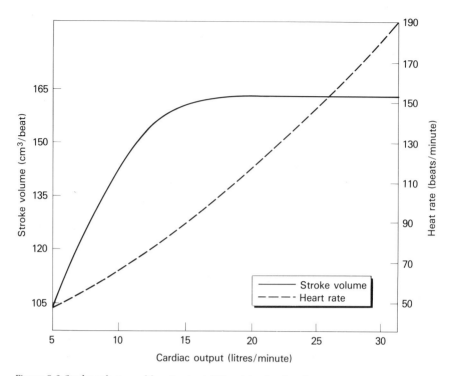

Figure 9.2 Stroke volume and heart rate at different levels of cardiac output in a marathon runner, from Guyton A. C., *Anatomy and Physiology* Saunders College Publishing (1985)

Vasoconstriction raises blood pressure locally, whereas vasodilation reduces it. *Overall* there would be a net decrease in blood pressure during dynamic exercise were it not for the increased cardiac output which results in a net increase in the systolic blood pressure (from 120 mm mercury at rest to as high as 180 mm mercury). This is the pressure recorded at systole, when the ventricles pump out blood. Diastolic pressure should remain more or less constant in a fit person at about 80 mm mercury.

Vasodilation in muscles

Blood flow through non-exercising muscles is extremely sluggish since the blood vessels are constricted. Constriction is achieved by the contraction of smooth muscle in the walls of arterioles and in the form of sphincter muscles at the points where the arterioles enter capillary beds. Capillary beds are networks of interconnecting capillaries. The sphincter muscles act as valves, able to shut off capillaries and divert blood through bypass vessels to venules. In response to exercise, vasodilation is brought about by nerve impulses from the sympathetic nervous system and from recently discovered nerve cells which have their nerve cell bodies in the walls of the arterioles. The vasodilation that continues after exercise during the recovery period is probably due to chemical factors such as higher levels of lactic acid and carbon dioxide, and lower levels of oxygen and pH.

As a result of vasodilation the blood flow in skeletal muscle is raised from about 5 cm³ to 80 cm³ of blood per 100 g of muscle per minute, in line with the up to 20-fold increase in oxygen demand.

Vasodilation of the coronary artery

The heart itself, being a muscle, also needs an increased oxygen supply during exercise. This it obtains by vasodilation of the coronary artery and greater blood pressure in the aorta forcing more blood into the coronary artery.

Removal of heat

Active muscle generates a great deal of heat energy. The amount of heat released is directly proportional to the amount of oxygen consumed, and the latter increases about 20-fold during maximal exercise.

Typically, a few minutes after exercise begins the rising blood temperature will be detected by the thermoregulatory centre of the hypothalamus and vasodilation of arterioles in the skin is stimulated via the medulla of the brain. This allows blood into capillary loops near the skin surface, facilitating heat loss.

Atherosclerosis

Lack of physical exercise is regarded as the fourth most important contributory factor to atherosclerosis after high blood cholesterol, high blood pressure and cigarette smoking.

Summary

Muscle requires about 20 times more oxygen per minute when at maximum activity than when at rest. This is achieved by increase in cardiac output, redistribution of blood to active muscles and greater unloading of oxygen from haemoglobin at low oxygen partial pressures (concentrations).

9.5 Monitoring physical fitness

Some of the important physiological measurements discussed in sections 9.2, 9.3 and 9.4 can easily be made. Some require special apparatus, but much of this is widely available in schools and colleges. Some of the useful items of equipment and their particular uses are summarised in table 9.2. Detailed instructions on how to use the equipment are not given here, only an indication of the variety and the uses to which the equipment can be put.

Many exercises and fitness testing routines have been devised and it is useful for a school or college and its students to have student records of performance. There is scope for useful project work by students in this area. A sample record sheet is shown in fig. 9.3. Some of the tests are described in the *Eurofit Handbook* on 'Testing Physical Fitness' produced by the Council of Europe, which has 21 member countries (see list of references at the end of this section). This includes details of a series of simple, relatively inexpensive standardised physical fitness tests which are being used throughout Europe in an international programme of fitness evaluation.

Table 9.2 Summary of some of the common apparatus available for recording physiological data.

Apparatus	Can be used to measure	Link with	Other points
Spirometer – records number and volume of breaths in a given time	Tidal volume (at rest and after exercise) Ventilation rate Pulmonary ventilation Vital capacity Timed vital capacity (forced expiratory volume – FEV)* Maximum ventilation volume (MVV)** Rate of oxygen consumption and hence metabolic rate Inspiratory reserve volume Expiratory reserve volume	Kymograph (mechanical) Up and down motion of lid can be converted to a voltage change by an electronic arm or transducer and the signal picked up by a chart recorder or microcomputer→VDU/TV or printer	Medical grade oxygen needed if lid is filled with oxygen (needed if more than a few breaths being recorded). Use with mouthpiece and nose clip. CO_2-absorber normally used in circuit to prevent rebreathing of CO_2. Subject must remain in one place but can be used with exercise bicycle or 'step test'.
Stethograph – records chest movements	Ventilation rate Qualitative changes in tidal volume	Tambour→kymograph Electronic manometer→chart recorder or microcomputer→VDU/TV or printer	Does not give actual volumes of air exchanged. Does not require mouthpiece and nose clip – therefore does not interfere with normal breathing. Effect of speaking/reading aloud can be observed.
Douglas bag – collects expired air in a given time	Oxygen uptake Volume of expired air produced per minute Expired air can later be chemically analysed, e.g. before and after exercise to find, for example, O_2 consumption or CO_2 production	Gas analysis equipment e.g. gas burette for chemical analysis of expired air Gas meter or spirometer if estimate of total volume required	Exercise more easily undertaken than with spirometer, e.g. can be used while running. Used with mouthpiece and nose clip. Can be used during exercise – particularly useful for measurement of oxygen consumption during vigorous exercise. Accurate. Simple.

Instrument	Measures	Output/Display	Notes
Peak flow meter	Maximum velocity of air flow during a forced expiration		Indication of lung disease and conditions causing bronchoconstriction, e.g. asthma, smoking
Oxygen meter	Oxygen content of inspired and expired air	Microcomputer→VDU/TV or printer; Chart recorder	Short term changes can be measured. Breath to breath analysis may be possible. Cheap, reliable instruments under development.
ECG (electrocardiogram)	Heart rate. Electrical activity of heart. Sinus arrhythmia if combined with recording of ventilation (speeding of heart during inspiration, slowing of heart during expiration)	Microcomputer→VDU/TV or printer; Chart recorder; Oscilloscope; Preamplifier→amplifier→loud speaker	Most reliable method for recording heart rate. Demonstrates PQRST cycle of electrical activity indicative of certain types of heart disease but interpretation requires medical expertise. Instant personal record of heart rate for data storage.
Sphygmomanometer	Blood pressure, e.g. changes in systolic pressure with exercise		Modern instruments rely on oscillometric rather than phonosensing. Fairly cheap (£50–£100) electronic devices available.
Pulse meter	Pulse		Battery operated. Reliability sometimes suspect.
'Sportstester'	Pulse	Could be linked with microcomputer but commercial software and interface expensive	More accurate than pulse meter. Radio signal from chest monitor and transmitter sent to a separate digital monitor which can be worn on the wrist, clamped to an exercise bicycle etc. Battery operated (check batteries replaceable).

Table 9.2 Summary of some of the common apparatus available for recording physiological data.

Apparatus	Can be used to measure	Link with	Other points
Bicycle ergometer, e.g. 'Monark 868'	Work load during exercise		Provides and quantifies exercise. Latter is important, particularly if comparing performances of different individuals. Energy output and oxygen uptake can be predicted with greater accuracy than for any other type of exercise. High motivator for training – enables targets to be set. No power supply needed. Relatively easily transported. Good ECG tracings can be obtained at the same time. Less accurate alternative is 'step test' (see text).
Skin-fold calipers	Fatness		Measures fatness rather than weight. Metal calipers give best results but plastic calipers are cheaper. Consistency of results obtained improves with practice – always take a mean.

*FEV: Subject first takes a maximum inspiration, then exhales as forcefully and completely as possible. Determine the percentage of vital capacity that is exhaled in 1 second. Normal figure for a 25 year old is about 80%. FEV is reduced if airways are constricted or obstructed, e.g. due to asthma, smoking.

**MVV: Breathe as rapidly and as deeply as possible over 15 seconds.
Healthy 25 year old man: range 100 to 180 litres/min   Mean: 140 litres/min
Healthy 25 year old woman: range 70 to 120 litres/min   Mean: 95 litres/min

The FITECH step test mentioned in fig. 9.3 is currently being used in over 1000 secondary schools in the U.K. and overseas as a simple measure of cardiorespiratory fitness for those aged 15 and above. It includes a cassette tape to work to. An aerobic fitness score and fitness rating are determined, based on age and pulse counts. The Physical Education Association (P.E.A.) are collecting FITECH test data from schools. Details of the test are available from Fitech Ltd. (see list of references).

Details of a fitness comparison survey being undertaken by P.E.A. are available from P.E.A. (see reference list). Some of the difficulties of standardising fitness tests are discussed in a *New Scientist* article of 23 February 1984 'Does Fit Mean Healthy?' (pp. 14–21, author Gail Vines).

PHYSIOLOGICAL DATA RECORD SHEET

FULL NAME ....M/F   DATE OF BIRTH ....

MAIN SPORT ....   AGE ....

POSITION/EVENT ....

STANDARD (College/County/Club) ....

OTHER SPORTS (Frequency) ....

DATE

HEART RATE   BLOOD PRESSURE
HEART RATE BEFORE EXERCISE*   SYSTOLIC
                                             DIASTOLIC

BODY MEASUREMENTS   FAT RECORDINGS
HEIGHT   TRICEPS
WEIGHT   BICEPS
% BODY FAT   SUB SCAPULAR
LEAN BODY WEIGHT   SUPRA ILIAC
FLEXIBILITY   TOTAL
SIT AND REACH*

EXPLOSIVE STRENGTH
STANDING BROAD JUMP*
SARGENT JUMP
SIT UPS (30 SECS)*

STATIC STRENGTH
RIGHT GRIP STRENGTH*
LEFT GRIP STRENGTH*

5 MINUTE STEP TEST (FITECH)
15 SECOND HEART RATE
FITNESS SCORE
RATING

CARDIORESPIRATORY ENDURANCE
12 MINUTE P.W.C. TEST USING BICYCLE ERGOMETER*

Figure 9.3 Sample physiological data record sheet. Dynamic strength, speed and balance tests could be added (see *Eurofit Handbook*). * Tests described in *Eurofit Handbook* (see text)

PWC$_{170}$ (Physical work capacity)

One commonly used test of aerobic or cardiovascular fitness is the PWC$_{170}$ test. It is based on the observation that heart rate response to exercise is a very good indicator of fitness level. As already noted, heart muscle is strengthened by exercise/training, thus increasing the efficiency of the cardiovascular system. PWC$_{170}$ is the physical work capacity (measured in watts per kg body weight) at a pulse rate of 170 beats per minute. The test can also be used to predict maximal oxygen uptake with a $\pm$ 10% error. The test is a widely used measure of endurance fitness, the body's response to sustaining steady state exercise. The rationale is that the fitter a person, the lower will be the heart rate in response to a given work load. Conversely, the fitter a person, the more work can be done at a given heart rate. One advantage of the test is that the person does not need to achieve maximal exercise and does not work to exhaustion. The administration of the test is described in detail in the *Eurofit Handbook*.

References

Testing Physical Fitness, Eurofit Experimental Battery Provisional Handbook, Sports Section of the Council of Europe, Strasbourg (1983).

Physical Education Association, Ling House, 162 King's Cross Road, London, WC1X 9DH, Tel: 01 278 9311.

British Journal of Physical Education published every 2 months, Journal of the P.E.A.

Fitech Ltd., Trafford House, Trafford Street, Chester, Tel: 0244 378811

North Staffordshire Polytechnic, *Health Related Fitness in the School P.E. Programme*: Introductory Concepts, 7 papers on the 'how', 'what', and 'why' of Health Related Fitness in schools

Lancashire County Council, *Health Related Fitness in the School P.E. Programme*: Discussion Document, includes details of tests as well as advice on implementing H.R.F.

Further Reading

AVERT/Health Education Authority (1988) *Learning about AIDS* (a project funded by AVERT to develop new ways of training AIDS educators; not suitable for use in unmodified form in school; much detailed information; uses group work, case studies and role play)

Clegg, A. C. & Clegg, P. C. (1973) *Man against disease*, Heinemann

COMA Report (1984) *Diet and cardiovascular disease, Committee on medical aspects of food policy*, DHSS Report on Health and Social Subjects no. 28 HMSO

Davies, B. M. (1984) *Community Health and Social Services* 4th ed, Hodder and Stoughton

Flora project for heart disease prevention (1978) *Diet and heart disease* (study pack of resource material)

Harvey, I. and Reiss, M. (1987) *AIDSFACTS* (revised edn.) Cambridge Science Books, (a pack to facilitate teaching about AIDS to 13–19 year olds; a wide range of teaching methods is included; comprehensive treatment of all aspects of the disease)

Inchley, C. J. (1981) *Immunobiology* Studies in Biology, 128 Arnold

Lamb, D. R. (1984) *Physiology of exercise*, Macmillan

Mackean, D. and Jones, B. (1985) *Human social biology* 2nd ed, John Murray

Macmillan guide to family health, ed. Tony Smith, (1982) Macmillan

Mandal, B. K. & Mayon White, R. T. (1984) *Lecture notes on the infectious diseases*, 4th ed, Blackwell

NACNE Report (1983) National Advisory Committee on Nutrition Education, Health Education Council

New Scientist AIDS monitor for regular updates on AIDS

Nicol Thin, R. (1982) *Lecture notes on sexually transmitted diseases*, Blackwell

Office of Population Censuses and Surveys (OPCS), London, (for up-to-date statistics)

Open University Course U205 *Health and disease* (1984, 1985), nine books, including *Health and disease, Studying health and disease, The health of nations*

Open University *Guide to healthy eating* (1985) Rambletree Publishing, produced by the Open University, Health Education Council and the Scottish Health Education Group

Pinching, A. J. (December 1987) *AIDS and the AIDS virus (HIV): Facts and implications, School Science Review* (ASE), 69, 205–16, (good on social issues as well as biological facts)

Phillips, R. S. (1983) *Malaria*, Studies in Biology, 152, Arnold

Roitt, I. (1980) *Essential immunology* 4th ed, Blackwell

Royal College of Physicians (1983) *Health or smoking?* a follow-up report, Pitman

Science in Society: Book A: *Disease and the doctor*, Book B: *Population and health*, Book C: *Medicine and care* (1981) Heinemann/ASE

Scientific American *What Science knows about AIDS* 259, 4, October 1988, Sci. Am. Books Inc. New York, USA

Shillingford, J. P. (1982) *Coronary heart disease, the facts*, OUP

Taylor, S. and Jordan, L. (1986) *Health and illness* (Social policy today series), Longman

Wingate, P. (1976) *The Penguin medical encyclopaedia*, Penguin

World Health the magazine of the World Health Organisation, 10 issues per year from WHO, Avenue Appia, 1211 Geneva 27, Switzerland or large bookshops.

Index